# Profit

## Without Oppression

### A BLUEPRINT FOR BUILDING
### AN ANTIRACIST ORGANIZATION

# KIM CRAYTON

# 13TH & JOAN

For permission requests, write to the publisher, addressed "Attention: Permissions Coordinator," 205 N. Michigan Avenue, Suite #810, Chicago, IL 60601. 13th & Joan books may be purchased for educational, business or sales promotional use. For information, please email the Sales Department at sales@13thandjoan.com.

Printed in the U. S. A.

First Printing, December 2022.

Library of Congress Cataloging-in-Publication Data has been applied for.

ISBN: 978-1-953156-82-2

# Dedication

Defining moment: my dad's death bought me my FREEDOM. He left me just enough money to feel comfortable enough to discover and follow my dreams but not enough to take his gift of FREEDOM for granted.

This book is dedicated to my family and friends who see, accept, and nurture my uniqueness and to future generations of entrepreneurs who desire to build businesses that are rooted in building a supremacy, coercion, discrimination, and exploitation FREE future.

This will NEVER be a complete list of folx who became my community and helped me make the transition from education into an unfamiliar technology world:

- Brandy Porter
- Alianor Chapman
- Alicia Carr
- Chris Aquino
- Toby Ho
- Angel Banks
- Beth Lang
- Bronwyn Morgan
- Chad Loder
- Dr. Danielle Smith
- Dr. Brandeis Marshall
- Dr. Elenor Seaton
- Erica Stanley
- Gloria Hall
- Gregor Martynus
- Jamie Frank
- Melva Steps
- Peter Aitken
- Ptah Dunbar
- Kathleen McMahon

- Barbara Hurd
- Twila Dang
- Trey Hunner
- Melanie Arbor
- Tracy Hinds
- Bryan Hughes
- Sareh Heidari
- Kristen Seversky
- Mark Tomlinson
- Jan Lehnardt
- Jessica Rose
- Josh Glover
- Sandra Persing
- Peter Müller
- Paula Gearson
- Tanya DePass
- Doc Parsons
- Paul Campbell
- Shireen Mitchell
- Bernadette Harris
- Jabari Adisa
- Saron Yibarek
- Robert Frelow
- Karl Phillips
- Eric Normand
- Ashley Hunsberger
- Jason Huggins
- Marcus Merrell
- Simon Mavi Stewart
- #causeascene Monthly sponsors
- #causeascene Community Volunteers
- #causeascene Podcast Guests
- and The Future Is FREE Monthly Sponsors

## Help Power The Movement 6-Month Supporter

These are the folx whose financial support allowed me to focus for 6-months on bringing this book to life:

- Michael Hartington
- Nathanael J. Strong
- Pete Holiday
- Diane Burnham
- Benjamin Niccum
- Rahul Gupta
- Garrett H. Dimon
- Amy Gebherdt
- Evan Schultz
- Jan Lehnardt
- Noel Baron
- Ken Ball
- Cameron Watters
- Joseph S Grossberg
- Steven M Silvester
- Kathleen McMahon
- Nader Dabit
- Krishna Kunche
- Karla L. Monterroso
- John Breen
- Steve Grossi
- Stephanie Miller
- Rebecca König
- Paula Gearon
- Jesse Jacob
- Erik Riedel
- Vincent Riemer
- Greg Philip
- Jeremy Hill
- Erin Mills
- Angie Jones
- Tamare Temple
- Forthright LLC
- Angela Pinney
- Douglas King
- Jordan Louis Sissel
- Hannah Howard
- and Steven Langbroek

# Acknowledgements

- Lauren Fisher
- Erin Mills & Strat House Team
- Shev Rush
- 13th & Joan Publishing House
- Andaiye Taylor
- Gabor Javorszky
- Paul Kinchla
- Angela Aquino
- Jordan Strauss
- Debs Durojaiye
- and Juliette Mothe

# Contents

# Foreword: Crucial Voices, Crucial Processes

*At the end of the day, my job is
to represent community.*

I was serving on the Stack Overflow board, where my mandate was to represent the community of the popular developer website when I met Kim. From the first time we talked, she had a clear vision of what she wanted to see the company doing to improve our businesses. It's one thing to have a strong internal moral compass to drive you, but when you're building a community for all the world's developers, it's another thing to have someone push to help us accomplish exactly that. She keenly understood the structural, organizational, and systemic constraints preventing us from having a more inclusive environment. This was not about one person's experience but about the experience of everyone involved, and in our conversations, Kim wasn't advocating for what she wanted; she was articulating a way of including *everyone*. After that experience, we stayed in contact mainly through social media, and she eventually invited me to talk on her podcast. It was a good way to get me out of my comfort zone. It was one of those moments you were being called in to talk about something you are well acquainted with, but I could tell Kim had a very strong understanding of where I was coming from. That was really what drew me into Kim's orbit. Here is this woman calling out how this company and community could be doing better. Because of how she did that, I was just inspired by her and wanted to be involved in whatever she had going on. We had different starting points, but we both had arrived at similar ideas about how the whole tech industry could be changed for the better. I think Kim's voice is crucial in pursuing that change. She has a profoundly effective way of communicating exactly how that change should come about.

## How necessary do you think voices like Kim's are when it comes to addressing these issues and concerns?

I think it is incredibly necessary. Many people have the right goal and intentions in mind, but as Kim says "Good intentions are often not good enough." I think you have to have a real *theory* on how you will apply pressure to the system to make it improve, but the ability to turn theory into action is rare. That's where Kim comes in; she can galvanize movements and bring out the people who are receptive to that message and then push them to make the changes. Now she could do it all herself, but that is the impressive thing about her; she has no ego about it. It's not like she is saying, "Got to put my name first," but to make people realize it is a bigger movement than any one person. Any movement needs people who understand when it's time to step aside and let others take the lead, and Kim is that person.

## What is the detriment of not having profound voices?

Without clear voices like Kim's leading the way, we end up on a path to moral failure. We as humans must strive to do right and ask ourselves what is right for those with the least and those who are most vulnerable. I want people to start there because I think so much of this conversation becomes about companies, organizations, and businesses when it needs to start with people. When I met Kim and most of the time since, I have been a CEO or on the board of, in some cases, multi-billion dollar companies. Their business case for inclusion is obvious, documented, and inarguable. And yet many of these organizations will compromise on their potential business or monetary value because they are not being as inclusive as they aspire to be. It's extraordinary when you consider how often companies do this. The biggest companies in the world will be turning away potential customers, revenue, opportunity, and growth by not following through on their own efforts to be inclusive. The simple fact that inclusion reduces the risk for your organization is often not persuasive enough for them. So, it becomes even more important to reach out to like-minded people and build a coalition of people who care about this moral imperative. Many good people get into technology or any business with an optimistic view and a drive to build cool things, bring value to people, and make their lives easier. And that's great! But we need to find a balance that will hopefully shift into more good than bad. We must remind these people building these cool things that make our lives more convenient, connected, or entertaining that they also have a moral obligation. Keeping this in mind, I believe it will make their work richer and have their work experience, creativity, and community shine brighter. It's not just about scolding bad behavior or shaming those causing harm; as we can see, that no longer works. It is about lifting, rewarding, and amplifying the people and organizations that do the right thing.

## What are some of the historical constraints you see that will make what we are addressing an uphill climb?

I think the first is the framing of the argument that Kim brings to bear. So many of the most effective activists challenge the authority of people who are used to being in that central power role. These people are used to being in power and view challenges, even positive challenges, as a threat. It puts them on the defensive, and they often lash out violently, literally and metaphorically, and that's the hardest part. For example, we can learn from open-source software in the tech world. One of the greatest and kindest things a person can do in an open-source environment is to say, "I looked at your code and found a bug." Or, "I looked at your software or app and found a bug." A bug report is an act of *generosity*. In a political context, if we look at the positive aspects of how the Constitution was framed, the idea that it could be amended was premised on the idea that it has bugs and needs to be fixed from time to time. It was supposed to be an act of generosity to participate in civic discourse to fix our legal system. Yet this exact same act of kindness is not always viewed that way by many tech companies when it happens in the realm of inclusion. You are seen as a hostile enemy. Again look at companies like Facebook and Google; if you say to them, "Hey, I found a security bug in your web browser," they give you a cash prize. They call it a "bug bounty," and they say "Thank you" for having found a potential security risk. Now, if you take the exact same scenario, but you are reporting a *cultural* risk instead of a security risk, a social risk instead of a technical risk, they will vilify you. If you work with them, they may even fire you, blacklist you, or ostracize you, which is an extreme escalation for something that should otherwise be a generous thing to do. However, one of the things that give me hope is the lesson we can take from what's happened in security. People who reported security bugs 20 years ago were treated as dangerous, scary hackers. They would get reported to the Feds and were demonized for simply reporting bugs until they eventually established a new set of norms and a cultural practice where reporting a bug was seen as a kindness. Tech culture made a real change, it did happen in this one area, so it makes me think that it is possible to shift the culture. Maybe it is possible that someone who reports a culture bug is welcomed for helping instead of being vilified.

## Do you believe that people are afraid to speak out because of vilification?

It's that threat of vilification that makes people afraid to speak out. The workers, community members, and ordinary people who don't have the authority and privilege are afraid they will be prosecuted, marginalized, or lose their jobs. And frankly, they are afraid for a good reason. These things *have* happened to people, so there is tremendous fear about speaking out for those who are vulnerable.

The extraordinary thing is, is if you take the most powerful executives, investors, and people on the board, they are afraid *too*. They feel they do not have power. Some of that is they have been working each other up into feeling like victims, but it's broader than that. They understand that culture has shifted.

Even the well-intentioned people in power are like, "I know the world is changing, but I don't know what it is changing into, and I don't know how to navigate this new world." When you are a captain of industry, you are this powerful, wealthy person everyone looks up to. It's terrifying to admit that maybe you don't know what will happen next. People too often have a mindset that says, "Well, I am rich, so I must be smart." If you tell them that they don't know something, it can threaten them a lot. The people at the lower end of the hierarchy are scared because they will be victimized if they point out that the system is broken. But the surprising part is that the people with the power often agree, maybe not to the same degree, but they understand something is *broken*. But they are afraid to address it because they don't know how to make a change, and then everyone ends up just sitting and waiting, hoping everything works out. This stuff takes work, sometimes, it takes self-reflection, and I think that is one thing that Kim has repeatedly pointed out at the organizations I was involved with or was a CEO of. We all want to think that we are good people, but there comes a time when you need to sit with yourself and reflect personally and professionally, and it is not always easy to do. Then also, this does not happen on the schedule you predicted; it comes when it comes, whether on social media or during a conversation with a coworker. Nobody puts it on their calendar, "Oh, three weeks from now, the world is going to go through this huge cultural change, and I am going to have to self-reflect on how I am going to change the direction of my business." It is forced upon you when you least expect it. It always feels like, "Wait, I was going to get to that, but I had this other stuff to do first."

The easiest thing to do is procrastinate when confronting your privilege.

## Why should people listen to Kim?

The world is changing, and you need to know where it will take you and how; that's just reality. Many people are walking around in denial right now, and that is not going to get you anywhere. You will be left behind if you stay in that denial while the world around you changes. Another reason people should listen to her is you will not find people who are the combination of truthful and principled as Kim is. She is a very savvy person in regard to systems, institutions, and organizations. It's a rare combination because the role of an activist is to be provocative and structurally antagonistic, but that's very rarely coupled with understanding how organizations change, how people change, and what motivates people to *want* to change. I think Kim's desire is that one day this is just something everybody does routinely, but for right now, it's still incredibly rare. That's what makes Kim so special; she is a person who unlocks a different potential. She is disciplined and principled in advocating for those who are vulnerable. She has their back and is so smart and knowledgeable about how organizations work that those in power can trust that she will advocate for ideas that are real and doable. Her ideas are grounded in principles that are practical enough that you can measure your progress.

## What do you want to say to Kim?

This work is about being human, helping humans, and enabling people to be their full human selves. Part of being human is to falter. When you are doing this hard work, you get tired. When you face impossible odds, trying to change the wealthiest industries that have existed in the world and some of the most powerful people who have existed in the world, it would be impossible not to get tired, dispirited, fatigued, or worn down. You wouldn't be human if you weren't. If the entire mission is for us to allow people to be human, then it is necessary to have moments of doubt, it is necessary to falter, and I think that is hard to understand. It's part of the process, part of Kim's broader message. Just as every system is corrupt and faulty, and we need to work on it anyway, every person is weak and needs moments of doubt, time to make mistakes, and reckon with or reflect on things within themselves. I think that is the main point. It's like, okay, you can take a day or weekend to catch your breath, and then we get back to it and understand that the moment of doubt, frustration, and fatigue are part of the process and necessary. Speaking personally, it was one of the harder points in my career when Kim called me out because I felt it was complicated. For some of the stuff she called me out on, I had context that I felt offered a useful perspective, but it was also difficult because it was *right*. So you sit with yourself in a way that feels isolated, and that forces you to have a moment of self-reflection. You think to yourself, "This person is right and consistent, and they are saying I am in the wrong, and I have caused the organization to be in the wrong." Maybe you have the power to fix it, or maybe you don't, but regardless, it is a hard place to be. And then the question for me and every organization or person who reads this book is: Do you want to be defensive? Do you want to wallow in it and say I am the victim here because I was on the wrong side? Or do you think you can be the person who changes and thus be *part* of changing things? Do you look at that person who called you out as an ally working with you toward a broader mission, or are they your enemy? I am very grateful to say someone like Kim is someone I can look at and say I will be with you on this. I think this is a great gift; it doesn't *feel* like a gift at the moment, but you know, after some time passes, you realize you wouldn't be as much as you *could* be without someone pushing you.

*Anil Dash,*
*CEO of Glitch*

# Disclaimer:
# Freedom Is Never Free

*"We get there together or not at all."*

*- Kim Crayton -*

This is a blueprint. It is designed for you to take any of the pieces and create a blueprint for your organization. If you are looking for a book that tells you, step by step, what to do, this is not that book.

The layout and format of this book stem from strategic choices. I have left ample white space amidst these pages for you to write your thoughts along the way. It is these strategic choices that guide the work I do with my advising clients because there are no one size fit all solutions when ones role is to establish welcoming and psychological safety as an organizational imperative. Although I am an expert regarding the content of this book, you, the reader, are the expert in your business and I give you permission to mold its content to fit your needs as you do the work of building towards a supremacy, coercion, discrimination, and exploitation free future.

I wrote this book in order to address and eliminate the many valid, and not so valid, excuses for not getting to work.. This is your blueprint.

If you believe in any way, shape, or form that current systems, institutions, and policies are NOT designed to privilege the few at the expense of the many, then I encourage you to stop reading now because this book is not for you. I did NOT write this book to convince or convert and I have no desire nor will I engage in "debates" on the validity of my positions because my lived experiences, and that of a multitude of others, for generations, is more than enough. If, on the other hand, you believe that creating a welcoming and psychologically safe business culture is critical, and you want to do the work of creating a world where equity thrives, then keep reading.

Here's the reality I'm seeking for all of us:

- Supremacy-FREE
- Coercion-FREE
- Discrimination-FREE
- Exploitation-FREE

This book is just the beginning but also a culmination of years of work to this end.

## Why This Book?

1. Industrial Economy → Knowledge Economy
2. A product/service is NOT a business.
3. Mitigate potential risk/crisis issues
4. Better positioned to innovate, compete, and profit
5. The future of work is accommodations, not assimilation.

**Before you begin reading, be aware of how to immerse yourself in this content. The book features the following segments:**

- MY STORY
- MY TRUTHS
- TWEETS
- REFLECTIONS
- CASE STUDIES

## A Note About Twitter

Let me be clear that Twitter, for me, has been more than a social media platform. At times, it has been a way of life. I've bared my soul on Twitter many times. It has served as a domain for my thoughts to live and be set free. It's where I've built community. It is the home of link articles, facts, and as we often say, *receipts*. Due to the fact that Twitter only recently added an edit button, some Tweets may contain typos. These typos have intentionally been left in the book to communicate authenticity and to serve as a reminder that we are human, not perfect.

Most importantly, find joy in this body of work. It is the first of many offerings and a milestone in the journey toward equity.

## A Note About the Word Folx

I am often asked why I use the term "folx". Some use "folks" as a gender neutral term. I started using "folx" because "x" has become the gender neutral default, particularly where language is gendered i.e. Spanish Latino and Latina, Latinx is gender neutral. Also, governments are starting to include "X" as an option on documents and IDs. You will see this term throughout this book as well as my work as a representation of inclusivity.

# Introduction: The Future Is Free

*"Profit Without Oppression is fundamentally rooted in the understanding that inequity and harm are the results of individuals who benefit from navigating the world with a zero-sum perspective."*

*—Kim Crayton—*

For as long as I can remember, I've wanted to build a business. From a young age, I knew I had this entrepreneurial mindset, the ability to see a problem and devise several solutions. The problem I encountered was that I could never figure out the magic sauce. I never could figure out how to make that leap into the entrepreneurial world. Even with several mentors and the internet, it just did not come together for me for a long time. So I did what most people did and got a "regular job," the most recent of which was in the education field.

It was not until I got encouragement from one of my mentors that I decided to leave the education industry and focus solely on becoming an entrepreneur. However, I was still subbing on the side. Unfortunately, the money from subbing wasn't enough to help me reach my goals, so in April 2014, I enrolled in my Doctor of Business Administration program. By that June, I discovered that my dad had cancer, and in August, he passed. HHis passing hit me hard, and I needed time to re-evaluate certain things because I'd just lived through what I thought would kill me." with "His passing hit me hard, and I needed time to re-evaluate certain things because I'd just lived through what I'd always thought would kill me. By the time mid-September hit, I had finally decided what my next course of action would be. I sent my family and friends a text saying, "I'm leaving education and going into 'tech,' when I figure out what that means, I'll let y'all know." After that decision, everything started happening so fast. By October, I was already attending my first tech conference and was hooked. I was a newbie in it, so I had a lot to discover, but I knew that this was what I wanted to be involved in.

In 2014 things in tech were getting interesting, and I could see a change was coming because many folx in tech started focusing on what they thought was "DEI," particularly related to conference attendees and speakers. It was the first time that I heard powerful white dudes begin to talk about their privilege openly.

When 2015 rolled around, I was firmly set on the idea that I wanted to get involved with tech, but I still was a newbie who knew little about the industry. With my educational background, I knew that learning the language of tech was the first step to success, so I threw myself into learning programming languages. However, I quickly found that although the prevailing narrative was the simplicity of learning to code, especially alone, the reality was entirely different. Tech hadn't developed efficient and effective education solutions rooted in adult learning theory. The majority of the programs I tried were designed in ways that reflected that individual's preferred learning style or what was easiest for them to build.

In 2016, I started speaking about the need for mentorship, and because it was a time when more folx started seeing the benefit of more voices than just white dudes, I had many opportunities to speak. I soon found myself addressing all manner of subjects related to business development, business strategy, diversity, equity, and inclusion. I also quickly realized that most folx thought their DEI efforts were far more impactful than they were, and by the end of 2017, I was over the surface-level effort and wanted to make more of an impact. Honestly, I was over the promises with no follow through and just wanted to fuck some shit up.

In 2018, with nothing to lose, I started using #causeascene to call out all the harm and façades of inclusion I encountered. My intention became to strategically make white folx, particularly white dudes in tech, uncomfortable by forcing them to face the truth of the impact of their perspectives, decisions and actions, while also understanding that an information economy required DEI as an organizational foundation for innovation, competitive advantage, and profitability.

Fast forward to 2020, the pandemic and George Floyd forced folx to face the horrors that they'd been able to avoid, and after years of being ignored and/or cast as the "angry Black woman," folx were finally willing to listen. But I knew that it would be only a matter of time before they were distracted again, so I created the Being Antiracist series: Introduction to Being Antiracist, Being Antiracist at Home, and Being Antiracist at Work to assist white folx with learning the basics of being Antiracist, while minimizing the negative impact whiteness has on others, as they learn because far too many folx turned to white voices to help them deal with their white feelings instead of getting to work on discontinuing their ability to leverage and be complicit in the harming of others. For many, the global "racial awakening" was a distraction hampering them from getting back to "normal" rather than understanding that "normal" was the problem.

In 2021, I'd had enough. I'd experienced firsthand the lengths at which the systems, institutions, and policies of white supremacy and anti-Blackness were designed to survive any challenge and that there's no bottom when your only function is chaos and destruction. I decided that I was no longer putting new wine into old wineskins because I understood that "the master's tools would never dismantle the master's house." It was time for a shift.

I spent most of that year figuring out how to shift from #causeascene to "the secret of change is to focus all your energy not on fighting the old but on building the new," which led me to develop the Profit Without Oppression economic theory and The Future Is FREE movement. Building a successful business has always been a key to establishing oneself and future generations. Unfortunately, gaining the knowledge and skills needed has largely been the sole domain of the already powerful and privileged. Knowledge and skills are either handed down from generation to generation or acquired via an educational system and institutions that routinely exclude all but the already privileged and powerful. Knowledge, particularly in the information age, should no longer be hoarded by the select few. The ability and the opportunity to create something that enables you to take care of yourself and your loved ones should be available to anyone who chooses that path. No one should go into as much debt as I have to gain this knowledge and these skills. Certain groups shouldn't always be producers and everyone else consumers, and I'm no longer willing to wait for the powerful and privileged to realize the harm they're inflicting on others before change can happen. I want a future free of supremacy, coercion, discrimination, and exploitation, and I am willing to burn the house down to ensure that this future comes to fruition.

Although this book is not for everyone, it is without question the manifestation of a desire to rid the world of systemic oppression. This book is a long-awaited and transparent answer for those ready, willing, and able to address the societal imposed inadequacies and biases through real lenses. This book has not been composed with the intent to convince or convert doubters/critics and focuses only on those who understand the need for and desire change.

Its contents are the result of years of studying, training, and toil. It is my greatest hope that you will discover a mindset and a system to navigate your future. Amidst these pages is a collection of personal stories, anecdotes, systems, procedures, and processes for your consideration. This book is necessary.

*"My work isn't dismantling current systems, institutions & policies of exclusion & harm or clawing back 'wealth' stolen by the powerful & privileged...It's to move BEYOND the indoctrination of 'zero-sum' and to embrace a supremacy-, coercion-, discrimination- & exploitation-free future."*

*Kim Crayton*

# The Theory

What do houses have in common?

- a foundation
- a floor
- walls
- a roof

Every part of our current political, social, and economic systems, institutions, and policies are rooted in oppression. They require domination, theft, dishonesty, intolerance, and the harming of others as fuel to operate AND are designed to discourage and even crush any challenge.

As we face our uncertain future, some understand that systems, institutions, and policies designed to oppress are not only unethical and immoral but also unsustainable. The flaws that inherently exist when exclusion is the business model are increasingly being highlighted globally.

Profit Without Oppression is an economic theory based on the understanding that to advance in ways where harm is not treated as a necessary "cost of doing business," we must forge an entirely new path that leads to a supremacy-, coercion-, discrimination-, and exploitation-free future.

The next books in the Profit Without Oppression series are as follows:

- Lead With Love
- Manage With Care
- Mentor With Wisdom

# Traditional Business Model vs. Profit Without Oppression Business Model

There is no other way to say it: All business models have not been created equally. You will hear this statement in various ways presented throughout this book. To fully understand this, we must first be willing to unlearn much of what we have been taught about business development. Before you delve further into the text, take a moment to note below the significant differences.

## Traditional Business Models:

- Product/Service (P/S) first mindset
- P/S dictates organizational operations
- Scale at all costs
- Shareholder-value ONLY consideration
- P/S development guides decisions related to any core values

## Pros:

1. Tightly focused [attention; get to X (i.e # of sales/customers/units, IPO, etc.)]
2. Binary decision-making
3. Status quo; familiar
4. More easily resourced

## Cons:

1. Benefits the already powerful and privileged
2. Increased potential for crisis event/s
3. Shareholder ONLY focused harms; "facilitates siloed thinking"
4. Replicates systems, institutions, and policies (S/I/P) designed to exclude and harm
5. Efforts to minimize harm are often unsuccessful due to S/I/P that, by design, can't accommodate such initiatives i.e., DEI, codes of conduct, inclusive language, etc.
6. Inability to forecast and mitigate potential harm
7. P/S dependent
8. Market conditions have a greater influence and impact due to P/S ONLY focus.
9. P/S ONLY focused means that all eggs are in one basket, which influences and impacts decision-making
10. P/S ONLY means that everything that leads to increasing shareholder value is a potential option [rudderless; goes wherever the wind blows]

## Profit Without Oppression Business Models:

1. Human-centric first mindset

2. Core values dictate operations
3. Supremacy-, coercion-, discrimination-, and exploitation-FREE is the foundation
4. Stakeholder value-focused
5. Core values guide decisions related to P/S development
6. Operations over P/S

## Pros:

1. Considers stakeholder impact
2. Risk management strategy that prioritizes harm reduction
3. Decreased potential for crisis event/s
4. Provides alternatives to S/I/P designed to exclude and harm
5. Leverages lived experiences, particularly those from marginalized and vulnerable communities
6. Makes "No" easier ["Does this align with core values?"]
7. Permission to chart a new course; true innovation
8. Improved ability to forecast and mitigate potential harm
9. Not P/S dependent
10. Facilitates Organizational Hospitality

## Cons:

1. Takes longer to stand up
2. Has to consider and resolve P/S with stakeholder impact [a more complex decision-making process; can be uncomfortable and messy]
3. Few examples to follow
4. Harder to get resourced
5. Knowing that harm can only be minimized and not eliminated

# I: Know Thy Self

"Knowing who you are is the only true counter measure we have against systems, institutions, and policies which are designed to define us."

Kim Crayton

# My Story

*"Evolution is inevitable. If anything,
over the years, I became more of an
advocate for the most vulnerable."*

*-Kim Crayton-*

Kindergarten is the earliest memory I have of helping other folx. I was the kid who never slept. Instead, they put me to work during nap time because I would talk to everyone. If I wasn't going to sleep, I was going to talk. The staff knew they had to keep me busy, so they put me to work setting up the "after nap" snacks.

My mom told me this story recently about the time when I was four. I had memorized the entire holiday play. I said my part and was hanging out on the side of the stage until this little boy got on stage and couldn't remember his lines. She said I went out on stage, said his lines, and walked back off. I had no memory of this and found it both hilarious and comforting, which I tweeted about because it confirmed that I have always been this person; this is something I have always done. I have always advocated for the underdog. It was clear to me that I have always prioritized the most vulnerable.

I liked to share what I had or knew, and I often found myself "fighting" for other folx. Let me be clear: This isn't new behavior for me. This is how I've always been. I've always been the one to cause a scene. I didn't get in trouble much for "bad behavior," other than when I "talked too much." I got into trouble because I kept standing up for other folx. Nothing much has changed as an adult. I became even more of an advocate for the most vulnerable, which sometimes caused me harm. Now that I'm wiser, I know how important it is to turn my trouble-making into strategic action for maximum impact. My goal is not to burn out in the trenches like many others.

I've always been the one to comfort or support others, but I rarely received comfort or support in return, which often worked against me. When you're perceived as "strong," the presumption is that you don't need anything, that you can handle everything on your own, which is clearly false and causes the "strong" to suffer in silence.

For example, when I was in college, I was the only one with a car. When I drove folx around, I never got gas money or anything else in return. I could say that folx were taking advantage of me, but they weren't because I let them. I drove folx around because, at some point, helping others became an obligation, which became a problem for me. I needed to work on "knowing thyself" to figure out why I was doing things I didn't want to do just because other folx expected me to. I needed to change the expectations I had let others place on me. I mean, even with family and friends, I have had to change their expectations or assumptions about what I will do and how I will do it.

# My Truths

"I want peace, joy, and prosperity" has been my personal mantra, but the truth is that I came here to do this work. I came here to create Profit Without Oppression. I don't know why, but that's my truth because if it weren't, I wouldn't be so damn good at it. I wouldn't be able to look at things the way I do, bring it all back, and connect the dots. I do this work because I want to help create the future I want to see, and if I decide I don't want to do it anymore, I'll stop. But until then, I don't care what other folx think because this work feeds me.

Just like when I shut down the #causeascene community because it was no longer feeding me. It had actually reached the point where it was causing me harm. Some folx didn't understand. I didn't give a damn because I had to figure out how to align my mantra with my truth. I lost a lot of income because of that decision. The majority of the folx who sponsored that work didn't follow the shift to Profit Without Oppression, and that was how I was paying my bills; that was how I was making money. After I stopped #causeascene, that support went away, and it became clear that once again, I wasn't going to be supported at the same level as I help others. I have learned that most folx treat giving as transactional; give to receive. You give "A" in exchange for something of equivalent value. I see things a bit differently. Instead of giving to receive, I operate from a give to regive perspective. I give because I like how it feels and because I know that in doing so, I'm making space to receive from any number of sources. So doing this work, being able to give without worry of return, truly puts a smile on my face. I truly enjoy being able to help people achieve their personal and professional goals.

The truth is that I know I am a generous person, and I love to give. I love to give because I find so much joy in it. If I am at a restaurant, I might leave a $100 tip on a $20 check and walk away before the server realizes just because I know that person is going to be excited, that feeling you get. I still give a lot, but I do it when I want to; I no longer do it out of obligation or someone's assumption or expectation.

I have also come to recognize that the acquisition of new information is a dynamic source of power. To that end, I am a lifelong learner. I am always going down some rabbit hole to learn something. I am a multipotentialite to my heart. That is why I know so much about the most random things. If someone were to look at my daily viewing, they'd see that it's all over the place. In one afternoon, I will have watched a British mystery, some documentary about World War II, something else about the mafia, soap operas, news, and cartoons.

I also value my independence, my freedom above all else. The ability to move about the world in ways that work for me has been my greatest sense of pleasure and pain. Pleasure due to the sense of euphoria I feel when I'm showing up as my authentic self and pain during those times when being my authentic self is under attack. This is why I don't join anything. So if I was in a sorority and if someone asked, "Is it better than another sorority," I would be like, "No, it ain't, it's just a group, and it's no better than another group." That's why I don't do stan culture. When your person fucks up, you are not allowed to acknowledge that, to hold that individual accountable for inflicting harm. We cannot continue to have privileged folx deflecting from the harm they caused or expecting to be extended the benefit of the doubt by pretending they have the same lived experiences as the most vulnerable because they don't. Being able to acknowledge one's relative privilege is essential for adopting a harm-reduction perspective, which is one thing I am good at, knowing where my position of privilege is and making decisions where I want to move with that in mind because sometimes my privilege is a benefit in some spaces. At other times it is a detriment to myself and others.

# Our Truths

Not everyone is ready for the new generation of fearless leaders. If you fuck up their pronouns, you are getting called out, and they don't care. Gen X was the first to initiate the act of pushing back because baby boomers had assimilated as a necessary strategy for success.

I get it and appreciate the Oprahs and Al Sharptons of the world, but it's time for y'all to share your wisdom and cede the stage to these young folx who have the understanding, language, and lived experiences to lead tomorrow's revolution. They are not trying to assimilate because they know their value in an information economy and understand the marketplace needs them in order for organizational leaders to leverage their knowledge to innovate, differentiate, and gain a competitive advantage.

Historically, the folx who could leverage technology were white dudes who had access to this stuff when no one else did. So if you can develop a business idea that leverages technology, then you are ahead of the game. As calls for accountability increase, some of these privileged white dudes are becoming aware that they have been complicit in harming others and that they are also being harmed; they are not escaping the harm.

Right now, folx are working in places they don't want to work in because they don't have alternatives, or at least they do not believe they have alternatives, but this market is changing. The information is out there, and we now have a chance to start our businesses and build out our processes, policies, and procedures, and there's not a damn thing these folx can do to stop us. We have finally found our voices, and we are not going away. You cannot put the cat back in the bag once it has been let out. Assimilation is over and accommodation is now the new expected norm, and for all those businesses and CEOs not ready for it, they need to get out of the way because we are not playing, and it's a beautiful thing.

Folx are now openly expressing themselves in ways that showcase their authentic selves, and there's no level of legislation that will halt this forward momentum. However, the work is just starting because change is never easy, especially for those who are used to always being on top. Now that they see their unearned positions of power and privilege being threatened, they have demonstrated that they will go to extreme lengths to ensure the status quo is maintained. We must keep applying pressure. We must keep calling out harm. We must keep focusing on building supremacy-, coercion-, discrimination-, and an exploitation-free future if we want meaningful, impactful, and long-term change.

Business has always been dominated by a small group of wealthy and powerful people, much like a private club or clique. Because systems, institutions, and policies were made to help a small number of people, nothing changes if private or government interventions don't address and fix the fundamental ways in which leaving "others" out and hurting them is the point. Because exclusion and harm will happen, again and again, the kinds of changes that are needed to make people feel welcome and safe must come from the groups that have been excluded and hurt the most. These groups are willing to make the changes and not take any crap.

# Common Myths

The myth that only certain types of folx can build businesses is far too common. Folx don't understand that it's not because we don't have the ability; we have not been given the information we can turn into knowledge or the resources to activate the resulting ideas. You cannot give what you do not have. We have a lot of information, but it is garbage. If you look at Elon Musk's privileges and opportunities compared to mine, there is a significant difference. He had two college-educated parents, and I only had one. He comes from wealth and is a product of South Africa during Apartheid when Blackness was literally illegal. He had computer access and learned how to code at a time when I couldn't do that. His access to people, ideas, and resources doesn't make him "smarter," just advantaged. So, just because folx don't know something doesn't mean it is not something they can't learn, are not right for, or are not worth investing in.

# What You Need To Know

Kim Crayton ~ Antiracist Economist ~ She/Her
@KimCrayton1

What we're witnessing with Spotify TODAY is what many talked about YESTERDAY when they brought Rogan on...how would they handle it when "all speech is equal" is your business model...which always brings me back to my desire for the widespread adoption of the Guiding Principles

PROFIT WITHOUT OPPRESSION
## Guiding Principles:

Tech is Not Neutral, Nor is it Apolitical

Intention without Strategy is Chaos

Lack of Inclusion is a Risk/Crisis Management Issue

Prioritize the Most Vulnerable

@KimCrayton1

9:45AM · Jan 28, 2022 · Twitter for iPhone

**Kim Crayton ~ Antiracist Economist ~ She/Her** 🟤
@KimCrayton1

Here's an example why the
#ProfitWithoutOppression Guiding Principles
should be widely adopted within the industry

PROFIT WITHOUT OPPRESSION

## Guiding Principles:

Tech is Not Neutral, Nor is it Apolitical

Intention without Strategy is Chaos

Lack of Inclusion is a Risk/Crisis Management Issue

Prioritize the Most Vulnerable

@KimCrayton1

 **CNN** @CNN· Nov 16

Activision Blizzard confronted its second employee walkout in less than six
months after a report raised new questions about CEO Bobby Kotick's
knowledge of longstanding and widespread sexual harassment and
discrimination allegations at the company. cnn.it/3wSuk4E

8:24AM · Nov 17, 2021 · Twitter for iPhone

# Tech Is Not Neutral, Nor Is It Apolitical.

There's a reason that this is the first of the four Guiding Principles...it's because this false narrative has led business leaders to cause a great deal of harm. What folx who embrace the concept of a neutral and apolitical tech fail or refuse to understand is that since whiteness is the default, so too are their politics and biases. When everyone in the room has such similar lived experiences, there's seldom a need to grapple with the impact of political ideas and decisions. But that doesn't make the ideas and decisions neutral or apolitical...it just means that you're better able to forecast the personal toll or impact. Unfortunately, for far too many, our very existence is neither neutral nor apolitical. In fact, for many of us, our lives are made political by the very same systems, institutions, and policies that whiteness can leverage in service to itself. It is not until we can internalize this first Guiding Principle that we can ever pursue a path that inflicts less harm on the world.

**Kim Crayton ~ Antiracist Economist ~ She/Her**
@KimCrayton1

Tech is NOT neutral nor apolitical AND every job recruiting platform, that I'm aware of, is scaling bias, discrimination, and harm

7:39AM · Jun 23, 2021 · Twitter Web App

 **Kim Crayton ~ Antiracist Economist ~ She/Her**
@KimCrayton1

Let me state again, that "we're in a knowledge economy and no longer making widgets"

For tech to be such an "innovative" space, we spend far too much time hazing folx, rather than recruiting and retaining folx for the value of their lived experiences

 Jun 28

REALLY pissed that my bf's 1st coding interview experience was a 12 hour long timed set of 5 problems where they tracked if he tab'd out, had a built in search engine that blocked all stack overflow sites & the built in IDE was FULL of errors making debugging nearly impossible

5:57AM · Jun 29, 2021 · Twitter for iPhone

**Kim Crayton ~ Antiracist Economist ~ She/Her** 🖤
@KimCrayton1

I'm not a fan of any political party/ideology because it's ALL rooted in white supremacy & anti-Blackness

That said, it's telling that the world's richest man justifies leaving the party he once appreciated for its "kindness", for one the that openly targets & harms Black folx

9:58AM · May 21, 2022 · Twitter for iPhone

**Kim Crayton ~ Antiracist Economist ~ She/Her** 🖤
@KimCrayton1

Musk is an example that an "apolitical" tech ideology was complete bullshit

"Apolitical" i.e. libertarians, for mediocre, unremarkable white tech dudes has ALWAYS meant maintaining the status quo

"Apolitical" for everyone else has ALWAYS meant being harmed by unchallenged power

5:32AM · May 31, 2022 · Twitter for iPhone

**Kim Crayton ~ Antiracist Economist ~ She/Her** 🌐
@KimCrayton1

High Tweet: being indoctrinated in individualism/exceptionalism ideology has been an effective AND efficient strategy for ensuring that the collective/community values never firmly take hold

3:16PM · Jun 7, 2022 · Twitter for iPhone

# Intention Without an Accurately Informed Strategy Is Chaos

Many of us have "good intentions." We truly want to be our best selves and to be a positive force in the world, but "good intentions" are notorious for leading to unintended and harmful outcomes. Although your intentions may be borne out of a genuine desire to be of service, without a strategy, a way to manage and measure the processes and results, you've only done half the work. "Good intentions" are fine but its impact that matters, particularly if your intentions cause harm. Without a strategy, how do you understand the outcomes? How do you know for sure if A + B = C or if some other random variable played a part? Without a strategy, how do you replicate success and learn the lessons of failure? For far too long, business leaders have adopted the "move fast and break things" motto but without a strategy, we seldom stopped to ask "What did we break? How did we break it? How did we help? Who did we harm? And how do we make amends and move forward?" After witnessing the immediate chaos that ensued following Elon Musk's take over of Twitter, I am updating this Profit Without Oppression Guiding Principle to reflect the need that just any strategy isn't enough to stave off or minimize the potential for chaos. The strategy must be accurately informed. This means that as much relevant stakeholder insight as possible is collected and evaluated in order to develop strategic plan that helps fills gaps in your understanding and area of weakness. Without an the "accurately informed" piece, an ill-informed intention can ONLY lead to an ill-informed strategy, which leads to an ill-informed outcome and chaos.

**Kim Crayton ~ Antiracist Economist ~ She/Her** 🌑
@KimCrayton1

Diversity [recruitment] efforts that don't have an accompanying strategy for improving the lived experiences of Black and brown talent, means that your existing systems, institutions & policies, rooted in white supremacy, will cause harm & are barriers to inclusion [retention]

Jan 23

Universities are tripping over each  to recruit Black and Brown talent. We are in a "racial awakening" writ large in America, and specifically in academia. Pause.Breathe. Reflect. We have to come to terms with WHY our institutions have been so recalcitrant to diversity/inclusion.

6:26AM · Jan 23, 2021 · Twitter for iPhone

# Lack of Inclusion Is A Risk/ Crisis-Management Issue.

Zora Neal Hurston said, "If you are silent about your pain, they'll kill you and say you enjoyed it." So often in organizations, leaders interpret lack of dissent, pushback, or questioning, to mean that there's universal agreement. This perspective should be seen as the red flag that it is. When the privileged and powerful use the lack of voiced opposition as a measure of silent acceptance, they demonstrate their lack of understanding regarding silence, particularly among the marginalized and most vulnerable, as a strategy of retrenchment; of protection by keeping one's head low and covering one's ass. What these individuals fail to understand is that silence is often the first sign that folx don't feel safe enough to tell you the truth. And when folx don't feel safe enough to tell you the truth, their silence is rarely a signal of happy times ahead. In an organizational setting, silence is a leading indicator that something is wrong and folx have made the decision to withhold their concerns because they don't desire to become targets for those who will use that "truth" as a weapon against them. With this understanding, every organizational leader should be asking themselves, what potential risk am I missing or crisis that I don't see ahead that others may and how can I create and nurture an environment in which inclusion is the default and silence is not ignored?

 **Kim Crayton ~ Antiracist Economist ~ She/Her**
@KimCrayton1

Lack of inclusion is a risk, and increasingly a crisis, management issue

Old ways of CYA [cover your ass] no longer work with an informed and empowered workforce

> Aug 4
>
> So, following raising concerns to #Apple about #sexism, #hostileworkenvironment, & #unsafeworkconditions, I'm now on indefinite paid administrative leave per #Apple employee relations, while they investigate my concerns. This seems to include me not using Apple's internal Slack.

4:33PM · Aug 4, 2021 · Twitter for iPad

 **Kim Crayton ~ Antiracist Economist ~ She/Her**
@KimCrayton1

CORRECTION: Omissions and lack of inclusion DOES render people invisible

> **AP APStylebook** @APStylebook· Jun 23
>
> From our race-related coverage entry: In all coverage ... strive to accurately represent the world, or a particular community, and its diversity through the people you quote and depict in all formats. Omissions and lack of inclusion can render people invisible.

12:33PM · Jun 23, 2022 · Twitter Web App

**Kim Crayton ~ Antiracist Economist ~ She/Her**
@KimCrayton1

Org leaders are finding out the hard, because they NEVER listen, that lack of inclusion is a risk, and increasingly a crisis, management issue

As we collectively emerge from the IMPACT of a GLOBAL pandemic, where EVERYTHING was in question...many are now rejecting the STATUS QUO

---

· Jul 7

Personal news: I've decided to leave Stanford Med. I've been mulling over the decision for several months, but yesterday's thoughtful letter by ▮▮▮▮▮▮▮ resonated with me.

The last year has been eye-opening, and I'll write a longer thread at some point.

/1

---

11:30AM · Jul 8, 2021 · Twitter for iPhone

**Kim Crayton ~ Antiracist Economist ~ She/Her** 🌍
@KimCrayton1

So let me quickly AND simply break down this reversal in policy

@OnlyFans learned first hand what I mean when I say that a lack of INCLUSION is a risk, and increasingly a crisis, management issue when focusing ONLY on shareholder rather than STAKEHOLDER value

> 🔵 **OnlyFans** @OnlyFans· Aug 25
>
> Thank you to everyone for making your voices heard.
>
> We have secured assurances necessary to support our diverse creator community and have suspended the planned October 1 policy change.
>
> OnlyFans stands for inclusion and we will continue to provide a home for all creators.

10:25AM · Aug 25, 2021 · Twitter for iPhone

**Kim Crayton ~ Antiracist Economist ~ She/Her**
@KimCrayton1

## Lack of inclusion is a risk, and increasingly a crisis, management issue...

> **Deadline Hollywood** @DEADLINE· Oct 12
> Warner Bros. Discovery has performed a quick U-turn on its decision to close its Writers and Directors Workshops. The company has said that that the two schemes will be houses within WBD's Diversity, Equity, and Inclusion unit, in partnership with WBTV deadline.com/2022/10/warner...

2:24PM · Oct 12, 2022 · Twitter for iPhone

 **Kim Crayton ~ Antiracist Economist ~ She/Her**
@KimCrayton1

## Lack of inclusion is a risk, and increasingly a crisis, management issue

## Org leaders are learning the hard way, in REAL-TIME, the leverage that exists with an informed, probably didn't even consider that these folx were planning exits on back channels, and empowered workforce

>  Aug 10
>
> From a CEO:
>
> "We announced return to office plans on Friday. By Monday a large number of our best people resigned, all wanting remote work. We're rapidly reassessing our policy."
>
> Worker power

4:43AM · Aug 11, 2021 · Twitter for iPhone

**Kim Crayton ~ Antiracist Economist ~ She/Her ...**    @KimCrayton1
Let's Unpack…

Other than the fact that this headline is clickbait, this situation highlights the continuing problems we face as we work towards a supremacy, coercion, discrimination, and exploitation FREE future… namely DEI efforts

**Kim Crayton ~ Antiracist Economist ~ She/Her ...**    @KimCrayton1
Once again, something INTENDED to benefit the marginalized and most vulnerable has been bastardized and perverted by both the well-intentioned and by schemers looking for easy 💲

I'll start with the schemers first just because that's quicker…there have and will always…

**Kim Crayton ~ Antiracist Economist ~ She/Her ...**    @KimCrayton1
be individuals whose superpower is exploitation…they can spot weaknesses and points of potential failure a mile away and DEI, for many, has been a jackpot for those who seek to profit by over-promising and under-delivering or just flat out lying

These folx wouldn't be so…

**Kim Crayton ~ Antiracist Economist ~ She/Her ...**    @KimCrayton1
successful if the first group, the well-intentioned, we're better at positioning DEI as something greater than just "it's good for business" because that's just part of the story

I can admit that, early on, I too made this mistake

It wasn't until I began diving…

**Kim Crayton ~ Antiracist Economist ~ She/Her ...**    @KimCrayton1
into systems, institutions, and policies that drive business decisions and behavior, that I was able to identify where the disconnect was and why things in DEI spaces continue to go off the rails…it's the part of the conversation most folx, particularly white folx, don't/can't…

**Kim Crayton ~ Antiracist Economist ~ She/Her ...**   @KimCrayton1
address

It's ALWAYS the elephant in the room...so let me break it down

1. In the Information Economy, it is the transformation of information, through lived experience, into tacit knowledge that enables organizational leaders to innovate, differentiate, and compete

 **Kim Crayton ~ Antiracist Economist ~ She/Her ...**   @KimCrayton1
2. Maintaining the young, white dude status quo has proven to be a barrier to meeting organizational goals

3. The status quo is ROOTED in systems, institutions, and policies DESIGNED to include, elevate, and amplify "young, white, dudes", while excluding, silencing, and...

 **Kim Crayton ~ Antiracist Economist ~ She/Her ...**   @KimCrayton1
harming "others"

SIDE NOTE: We don't have young, white dude dominated industries by accident

4. Current DEI efforts don't fair well because there's been little success in getting young, white dudes to understand and acknowledge that they ARE the status quo and the need to...

 **Kim Crayton ~ Antiracist Economist ~ She/Her ...**   @KimCrayton1
move beyond such a narrow measure of "success"

Without this understanding, young, white dudes feel attacked; victimized

Now let's address the attached article...

Ideally, this individual, let's call him Mike, has consistently delivered what has been asked of him

**Kim Crayton ~ Antiracist Economist ~ She/Her ...**   @KimCrayton1
If past is future, Mike expects to be rewarded/compensated for his effort

At this same time, organizational leaders have "realized" [this is often very shallow] that to effectively compete, "they need to focus on DEI" and they are forced to look outside of their organization

**Kim Crayton ~ Antiracist Economist ~ She/Her ...**   @KimCrayton1
SIDE NOTE: Mike is still operating under the belief that he's gotten this job, and others, solely on merit...even if obtained via his networks, Mike "believes" that he wouldn't have been given the opportunity if he hadn't DESERVED it [status quo]

**Kim Crayton ~ Antiracist Economist ~ She/Her ...**   @KimCrayton1
Due to systems, institutions, and policies DESIGNED to privilege Mike, he never questions his professional trajectory AND he often attributes "others" lack of success to their individual failing, rather than being intentionally excluded

**Kim Crayton ~ Antiracist Economist ~ She/Her ...**   @KimCrayton1
Mike's a "good guy"; he's not racist

He would never discriminate against anyone...but what Mike lacks in his understanding is that, he doesn't have to discriminate, because the systems, institutions, and policies are DESIGNED to handle that for him

**Kim Crayton ~ Antiracist Economist ~ She/Her ...**   @KimCrayton1
Now, you have competing internal narratives going on at the same time (1) Mike "believes" that he has EARNED a raise/promotion/etc (2) organizational leaders understand, again at a very shallow level, that success REQUIRES DEI because the voices of only young white dudes, in...

**Kim Crayton ~ Antiracist Economist ~ She/Her ...**   @KimCrayton1
an information economy, means that you're exposing the business to "blind spots", which increase risk/crisis factors and decrease profits

35

(1) Mike's perspective is micro
(2) organizational leader's perspective is macro

This misalignment is a problem just waiting to happen

**Kim Crayton ~ Antiracist Economist ~ She/Her ...**   @KimCrayton1
So as organizational leaders search professional networks for "others" to add to the team thus enabling them to leverage DEI as an organizational strategy, they rarely have done the work to ensure that the Mike's within the organization understand

**Kim Crayton ~ Antiracist Economist ~ She/Her ...**   @KimCrayton1
SIDE NOTE: gaining understanding is NOT the same as seeking permission...it's merely an exercise in communicating organizational needs and effectively positioning DEI decisions not as "us vs them"

Without this "understanding" what organizational leaders view as vital...

**Kim Crayton ~ Antiracist Economist ~ She/Her ...**   @KimCrayton1
Mike views them as personal attacks, and honestly so would I if I weren't a Black woman who has the lived experience of whiteness being elevated above me no matter the documentation that would make such decisions nonsensical

**Kim Crayton ~ Antiracist Economist ~ She/Her ...**   @KimCrayton1
What Mike also doesn't understand is that organizational leaders, no matter how intentional, rarely will do what's needed to ensure that they're able to leverage DEI because other than creating the position, nothing within the organization, designed to prioritize...

**Kim Crayton ~ Antiracist Economist ~ She/Her ...**   @KimCrayton1
young, white dudes, changes...the same systems, institutions, and policies DESIGNED to exclude and harm remain intact

Can't plant tomatoes in toxic soil and not expect to be poisoned

SIDE NOTE: some times organizational leaders can leverage a "hire" rather than "replace" DEI...

**Kim Crayton ~ Antiracist Economist ~ She/Her ...**    @KimCrayton1
strategy but there're a lot of variables to consider

Now here's the hard part for Mike...still a white dude, he's s no longer young and now has become a "victim" of the same systems, institutions, and policies that previously benefited him...because he doesn't understand this...

**Kim Crayton ~ Antiracist Economist ~ She/Her ...**    @KimCrayton1
the ONLY enemy he sees, let's be honest, is allowed to target, are the "others"...because, Spot The Pattern...his whiteness enables him to ONLY be casted as hero/victim, never the villain

To summarize, DEI doesn't work because no one's being honest regarding...

**Kim Crayton ~ Antiracist Economist ~ She/Her**
@KimCrayton1

what led to the lack of diversity, equity, and inclusion in the first damn place...so to the Mike's of the world, DEI shows up like a "solution looking for a problem" and not the organizational imperative that it is

1:15 PM · Jun 11, 2022 · Twitter for iPhone

37

**Kim Crayton ~ Antiracist Economist ~ She/Her** 🌑 🌀
@KimCrayton1

Lack of inclusion is a risk, and increasingly a crisis, management issue AND we're at the start of seeing essential talent walk out of organizations, large and small, taking their untapped knowledge and skills with them

> 🗞 **The New York Times** @nytimes· Jul 21
>
> Maria Taylor, a popular ESPN studio host, has left the company, ESPN announced Wednesday.
>
> The departure had been expected since early this month, when The New York Times reported on disparaging comments made about Taylor by her colleague, Rachel Nichols. nyti.ms/3eJTmem

11:45AM · Jul 21, 2021 · Twitter for iPad

**Kim Crayton ~ Antiracist Economist ~ She/Her**
@KimCrayton1

Lack of inclusion is a risk, and increasingly a crisis, management issue

The shift is happening folx

Maintaining the status quo will now come at a cost to organizational success

> Jun 1
>
> I left Google last Friday.
>
> I will sorely miss my incredible colleagues and hope they one day get to enjoy an environment where they feel safe to take risks, be themselves and challenge the status quo.
>
> I have not decided what I will do next. I will take a break and rest for now.

1:56PM · Jun 1, 2021 · Twitter for iPhone

**Kim Crayton ~ Antiracist Economist ~ She/Her** 🖤 🤍
@KimCrayton1

Lack of inclusion is a risk, and increasingly a crisis, management issue AND we must ALL address our own internalized white supremacy and anti-Blackness because it's a GLOBAL issue

 **Lin-Manuel Miranda** @Lin_Manuel· Jun 14
-LMM

among the leading roles.
I can hear the hurt and frustration over colorism, of feeling still unseen in the feedback.
I hear that without sufficient dark-skinned Afro-Latino representation, the work feels extractive of the community we wanted so much to represent with pride and joy.
In trying to paint a mosaic of this community, we fell short.
I'm truly sorry.
I'm learning from the feedback, I thank you for raising it, and I'm listening.

4:28AM · Jun 15, 2021 · Twitter for iPhone

**Kim Crayton ~ Antiracist Economist ~ She/Her** 🏾
@KimCrayton1

Lack of inclusion is a risk, and increasingly a crisis, management issue AND some ideas need to just die at the thought bubble 💭 stage

7:48PM · Oct 13, 2021 · Twitter for iPad

41

**Kim Crayton ~ Antiracist Economist ~ She/Her** 🖤
@KimCrayton1

Lack of inclusion is a risk, and increasingly a crisis, management issue AND the landscape that has enabled tech to operate with little to no consequences is changing BUT without prioritizing the voices and needs of the most vulnerable, it'll just be more of the same shit

> ▓▓▓▓▓▓▓ Jun 11
>
> Big news out of Congress: House lawmakers have officially introduced five bipartisan bills that target the underlying business models of Silicon Valley giants and in some cases open the door to breakups.

1:02PM · Jun 11, 2021 · Twitter for iPhone

**Kim Crayton ~ Antiracist Economist ~ She/Her** 🖤
@KimCrayton1

Lack of inclusion is a risk, and increasingly a crisis, management issue AND white women, due to white supremacy and anti-Blackness, in DEI roles are often just an indication of troubles ahead

> ▓▓▓▓▓▓▓▓▓▓ Aug 5
>
> alright i'm in the waiting room at the vet and in the mood to throw more shade:
>
> awhile back a Head of People (well-pedigreed white woman) at [well-known startup] requested a meeting because they needed help with their DEI strategy.

10:59AM · Aug 5, 2021 · Twitter for iPhone

42

**Kim Crayton ~ Antiracist Economist ~ She/Her** 🙏
@KimCrayton1

Lack of inclusion is a risk, and increasingly a crisis, management issue

This also highlights my desire to have serious conversations related to #ProfitWithoutOppression because there continues to be a fundamental misalignment with stated and demonstrated organizational values

 · Jun 27

"We do not believe it is appropriate to judge members of Congress solely based on their votes on the electoral certification," a Toyota spokesperson said in a statement emailed to Axios.

9:44PM · Jun 27, 2021 · Twitter for iPhone

**Kim Crayton ~ Antiracist Economist ~ She/Her** 🙏
@KimCrayton1

Lack of inclusion is a risk, and increasingly a crisis, management issue that continues to damage the minds, bodies, and spirits of Black women

The is why understanding whiteness as mediocre and unremarkable is NOT a slur but is in fact REALITY

8:25AM · Sep 28, 2021 · Twitter for iPhone

43

**Kim Crayton ~ Antiracist Economist ~ She/Her**
@KimCrayton1

Lack of inclusion is a risk, and increasingly a crisis, management issue AND Black women are the Kryptonite to white supremacy and anti-Blackness

> 𝕿 **NYT Business** @nytimesbusiness· Jun 23
>
> The journalist Nikole Hannah-Jones told the University of North Carolina that she will not join its faculty as planned unless she is granted tenure. A letter from her lawyers said an unnamed "powerful donor" had contributed to her tenure being denied. nyti.ms/3xKU4iO

8:02AM · Jun 23, 2021 · Twitter for iPhone

 **Kim Crayton ~ Antiracist Economist ~ She/Her**
@KimCrayton1

Lack of inclusion is a risk, and increasingly a CRISIS, management issue AND BLACK WOMEN ARE ALL OUT OF FUCKS AND ARE CHALLENGING WHITE SUPREMACY AND ANTI-BLACKNESS AT SCALE

Black women are SHOWING y'all that our collective liberation is through us

9:14AM · Jul 6, 2021 · Twitter for iPhone

**Kim Crayton ~ Antiracist Economist ~ She/Her** 🟤
@KimCrayton1

Lack of inclusion is a risk, and increasingly a crisis, management issue AND tech has pitched harming the marginalized and most vulnerable as a selling point

The California Department of Fair Employment and Housing has filed an explosive lawsuit against Activision Blizzard for discrimination. Some of the details in the complaint are horrifying

lso fostered a pervasive "frat bo... another example, a female employee who worked at Blizzard E... r level, denied equal pay, and passed over for a promotion des...

women are subjected to "cube c... earned it: (1) highly rated performance reviews; (2) she gener... er marketing campaigns than her male counterpart; and (3) she

as they "crawl" their way throu... is her male counterpart. Despite her accomplishments, her mal... nthly or weekly one-on-one meetings with the Vice President.

behavior toward female employ... ie opportunities and unsurprisingly was passed over for a prom... art.

deo games for long periods of ti... iilarly, other female employees at Blizzard Entertainment were... equal pay and further delayed or passed over for promotions i...

ployees, engage in banter about... lacked the same experience or qualifications but who were frie... newly promoted male supervisor delegated his responsibilitie... vor of playing Call of Duty. Other male supervisors would ref...

ike about rape. yees, going to their male counterparts for information.

4:40AM · Jul 22, 2021 · Twitter for iPhone

**Kim Crayton ~ Antiracist Economist ~ She/Her** 🖤 🤍
@KimCrayton1

Lack of inclusion is a risk, and increasingly a crisis, management issue & whiteness will do whatever it has to in order to remain relevant & in power...take care of each other because white supremacy has NEVER been challenged at this scale & this is just the beginning

> ████████████████████████████████ | Jun 15
>
> So, I wrote this about @nhannahjones and the court case that @Sifill_LDF and @NAACP_LDF are helping her with.
>
> The conservative haters are mad, obviously...
>
> charlotteobserver.com/opinion/articl...

1:13PM · Jun 15, 2021 · Twitter for iPhone

 **Kim Crayton ~ Antiracist Economist ~ She/Her** 🖤 🤍
@KimCrayton1

lack of inclusion is a risk, and increasingly a crisis, management issue AND I'm wondering what it will take for y'all to start having serious conversation related to #ProfitWithoutOppression

>  Sep 27
>
> "My definition of success has changed." How women are re-evaluating what they want from work—and life. on.wsj.com/3of9fz4

8:12PM · Sep 29, 2021 · Twitter for iPad

**Kim Crayton ~ Antiracist Economist ~ She/Her**
@KimCrayton1

Lack of inclusion is a risk, and INCREASINGLY a crisis, management issue AND organizational leaders are finding very hard to stay silent, as they once did, when the problematic folx they "endorse" cause problems

 **boohooMAN** @boohooMAN· Jul 28

boohooMAN condemn the use of homophobic language and confirm we will no longer be working with DaBaby.

Diversity and inclusion are part of the boohoo Groups DNA and we pride ourselves on representing the diverse customers we serve across the globe.

1/2

> homophobic language and confirm we will no longer be working with DaBaby.
>
> Diversity and inclusion are part of the boohoo Groups DNA and we pride ourselves on representing the diverse customers we serve across the globe.
>
> We stand by and support the LGBTQ+ community, and do not tolerate hate speech or discrimination in any form.

1:28PM · Jul 28, 2021 · Twitter for iPhone

# Prioritize The Most Vulnerable.

With an understanding of the first three Guiding Principles, it makes sense that prioritizing the most vulnerable becomes the goal. As existing systems, institutions, and policies that were designed to include and advantage the few at the expense of the many continue to be exposed, it's clear that righting the harm of the past isn't achieved by pursuing a notion of "equality" that has never existed. It is instead time to turn our attention and resources on understanding and amplifying the needs and well-being of those who, through circumstances not of their own creation, have developed ways to navigate the intentional and targeted harm they encounter on a daily basis. When we prioritize those who've had the lived experiences of exclusion and exploitation, we gain insight into situations and circumstances, particularly potentials for harm, that can become the foundation on which to develop innovative ideas and solutions to complex problems that are often unknown to those outside those targeted communities.

**Write/Speak/Code**
@WriteSpeakCode

"If you have white privilege and you aren't willing to risk anything, you're not doing the work. Privilege is about access. You may not realize you have privilege when you have always had access. Prioritize the most vulnerable." - @KimCrayton1, keynote speaker of #WSC2019Conf

11:11AM · Aug 18, 2019 · Twitter Web App

**Kim Crayton ~ Antiracist Economist ~ She/Her** 🖤 🤍
@KimCrayton1

I'll leave this right here...

"The employee, who is Black and currently pregnant, asked not to be named for fear of online harassment."

Not a good look @netflix

This is why we must prioritize the most vulnerable & why we need to operate through a #ProfitWithoutOppression lens

> 🔽 **The Verge** @verge· Oct 15
> Netflix just fired the organizer of the trans employee walkout
> theverge.com/2021/10/15/227...

3:00PM · Oct 15, 2021 · Twitter for iPhone

**Kim Crayton ~ Antiracist Economist ~ She/Her** 🖤
@KimCrayton1

This is a nuanced topic but focusing on how Black folx engage with each is a distraction because it doesn't account for the MAJORITY of white folx in tech who're doing absolutely nothing to prioritize the most vulnerable

4:04PM · Jun 2, 2021 · Twitter for iPhone

**Kim Crayton ~ Antiracist Economist ~ She/Her** 🖤
@KimCrayton1

This is why leaders who delude themselves that lack of OVERT conflict is an indication of organizational harmony are often facilitators of professional violence

De center the privileged to prioritize the most vulnerable to understand what's really going on with stakeholders

> Jun 4
>
> I once had a tech CEO tell me "I'm terrified you are telling me there could be racist groups organizing across my company" and I said "Start a very public diversity initiative and you will not wonder, you will know, they will make themselves heard.

8:08PM · Jun 4, 2022 · Twitter for iPhone

**Kim Crayton ~ Antiracist Economist ~ She/Her**
@KimCrayton1

This is what happens when org leader's words of inclusion DO NOT match their actions to minimize harm & prioritize the most vulnerable

As legislation that challenges the humanity of non cis, hetero, Christian, white dudes pass, the more business leaders will feel the heat

PROFIT WITHOUT OPPRESSION

# Guiding Principles:

Tech is Not Neutral, Nor is it Apolitical

Intention without Strategy is Chaos

Lack of Inclusion is a Risk/Crisis Management Issue

Prioritize the Most Vulnerable

@KimCrayton1

 **The Hollywood Reporter** @THR· Mar 7

Disney CEO Bob Chapek Addresses Company's Response to Florida's 'Don't Say Gay' Bill hollywoodreporter.com/business/busin...

6:53PM · Mar 7, 2022 · Twitter for iPhone

**Kim Crayton ~ Antiracist Economist ~ She/Her** 🌍
@KimCrayton1

Tech is NOT neutral nor apolitical and many of the decisions being made by mediocre, unremarkable, white dudes in tech lack the nuanced perspectives needed to minimize harm and to prioritize the most vulnerable

This appears to be a change from an earlier position when the company said it would not label the personal accounts of heads of state since such accounts already have "widespread name recognition, media attention, and public awareness."

🔽 **The Verge** @verge· Feb 12

Twitter plans to label the personal accounts of heads of state

1:44PM · Feb 12, 2021 · Twitter for iPhone

53

**Kim Crayton ~ Antiracist Economist ~ She/Her** 🖤 🤍
@KimCrayton1

This is why I now focus on highlighting problematic and harmful systems, institutions, and policies because, in my experience, when that voices that prioritize the most vulnerable are removed from the conversation, that void is then used to justify these decisions and behaviors

>  Jun 11
>
> It's impossible to convince someone that something won't work when they have a financial incentive to disagree with you.
>
> But telling them I told you so afterwards is counterproductive and mean spirited.
>
> With that insight, I'm taking a break from talking about crypto & web3.

5:10AM · Jun 11, 2022 · Twitter for iPhone

 **Kim Crayton ~ Antiracist Economist ~ She/Her** 🖤 🤍
@KimCrayton1

Tech is NOT neutral nor apolitical AND we have to challenge those systems, institutions, and policies that don't prioritize the most vulnerable

>  **NY AG James** @NewYorkStateAG· May 10
>
> I'm calling on @Facebook to abandon its plans to create a version of @Instagram for children under the age of 13.
>
> This is a dangerous idea that can be detrimental to children and put them directly in harm's way.

8:57AM · May 10, 2021 · Twitter for iPhone

54

**Kim Crayton ~ Antiracist Economist ~ She/Her** 
@KimCrayton1

Just what we need, another mediocre, unremarkable, white dude in tech with no ethical compass to prioritize the most vulnerable...who in fact, DEMONSTRATED that he operates from a "the harm is the point" ethos

> **The Daily Beast** @thedailybeast· Jun 11
> One of Donald Trump's most loyal foot soldiers, Jason Miller, is set to leave the Trump sphere to become the CEO of a new tech company

12:30PM · Jun 11, 2021 · Twitter for iPhone

**Kim Crayton ~ Antiracist Economist ~ She/Her** ⬤... @KimCrayton1
I'm increasingly aware of how I'm managing my life through the lens of the Guiding Principles

Ex: my vaccine hesitancy [to be clear, I didn't doubt the science. I prefer naturopathic remedies over pharmaceuticals whenever possible, so...

PROFIT WITHOUT OPPRESSION
## Guiding Principles:

Tech is Not Neutral, Nor is it Apolitical

Intention without Strategy is Chaos

Lack of Inclusion is a Risk/Crisis Management Issue

Prioritize the Most Vulnerable

@KimCrayton1

**Kim Crayton ~ Antiracist Economist ~ She/Her** ⬤... @KimCrayton1
I'd decided to continue to self-quarantine for the Summer and access the situation beyond Labor Day]

1. Tech is not neutral, nor is it apolitical: since this is now my default, I understand that technology is often used for unintended, and often harmful, purposes...

**Kim Crayton ~ Antiracist Economist ~ She/Her** ⬤... @KimCrayton1
so I've learned to question "who benefits?" "who's using the technology to scale their ideas/messages and why?" "who's being harmed and how are these messengers addressing it?"

These kinds of questions force me to operate beyond the binary;

**Kim Crayton ~ Antiracist Economist ~ She/Her** 🍪... @KimCrayton1
they require BOTH quantitative AND qualitative data

It doesn't take long to determine that many of the arguments against the vaccine, and science in general, were rooted in white supremacy and anti-Blackness

 **Kim Crayton ~ Antiracist Economist ~ She/Her** 🍪... @KimCrayton1
2. Intention without strategy is chaos: once I've gathered enough information, I begin to formulate a strategy around my intended behavior

To continue my pre-vaccine behavior [staying home, having things delivered when possible, wearing quality masks and...

 **Kim Crayton ~ Antiracist Economist ~ She/Her** 🍪... @KimCrayton1
social distancing whenever I had to go out], while those who wanted to "get out" received the vaccine or stayed masked and enjoyed their Summer

I would reevaluate my decision as Labor Day approached...kids would be back in school and I'd made plans to visit my mom

 **Kim Crayton ~ Antiracist Economist ~ She/Her** 🍪... @KimCrayton1
3. Lack of inclusion is a risk/crisis management issue: it didn't take long to observe that things weren't going as well as folx had hoped and yet, folx were increasingly behaving is if they were

Each new variant introduced an unknown variable that caused way too...

 **Kim Crayton ~ Antiracist Economist ~ She/Her** 🍪... @KimCrayton1
many folx, for my comfort, to forget how science works...the whole hypothesis, test, evaluate, repeat cycle that we learned and understood no longer mattered

So instead of basing one's behavior on new information, folx just questioned the entire scientific/research process...

**Kim Crayton ~ Antiracist Economist ~ She/Her** 🌑... @KimCrayton1
which meant that the hypothetical conditions that were once thought
possible [a COVID-19 free Fall] was now out of the question BUT as
the number of cases, hospitalizations, and deaths began to rise
again, folx "post COVID-19 behavior" intensified

 **Kim Crayton ~ Antiracist Economist ~ She/Her** 🌑 🌑
@KimCrayton1

4. Prioritize the most vulnerable: the perfect
storm...as the COVID-19 numbers began to rise
again, there also were reasons for me to leave the
house, all related to me being around medically
challenged and vulnerable people that I care about
AND as the sense of comfort I once...

 Kim Crayton ~ Antiracist Economist ~ She/Her 🌑 🌑
@KimCrayton1

had related to the vaccines giving folx back a
"sense of normal" decreased, my level of anxiety
grew and was starting to get out of control, so I
reached out to ▓▓▓▓▓▓▓▓▓▓ for advice and
decided to get vaccinated AND still stick to my
pre-vaccine behavior, with the...

7:03AM · Sep 14, 2021 · Twitter for iPhone

**Kim Crayton ~ Antiracist Economist ~ She/Her** 🤎
@KimCrayton1

knowledge that things on the ground will continue to change as this virus mutates AND that I'll have to reevaluate my behavior accordingly until we're truly POST pandemic

**Kim Crayton ~ Antiracist Economist ~ She/Her** 🤎
@KimCrayton1

BTW...that trip to see my mom after Labor Day, whom I haven't seen since the end of October 2019, didn't happen because of folx increasingly ridiculous and violent behavior

There's currently no method of travel that I trust enough where the potential for harm is low enough for me

7:03AM · Sep 14. 2021 · Twitter for iPhone

**Kim Crayton ~ Antiracist Economist ~ She/Her 🖐️...** @KimCrayton1
I just had to post this in my pilot management training and I'm sharing because it's everywhere and happens right in front of y'all:

"Now I need to address a welcoming and psychological safety issue that I've observed...the majority of the engagement so far has been led...

**Kim Crayton ~ Antiracist Economist ~ She/Her 🖐️...** @KimCrayton1
and/or driven by Black women, which is unacceptable. Black women have been conditioned to do the work when others won't, because let's be honest, we'll be the first blamed for collective failure.

**Kim Crayton ~ Antiracist Economist ~ She/Her 🖐️...** @KimCrayton1
How this *behavior* appears to be on autopilot is an example of what I mean when I post "systems, institutions, and policies of white supremacy and anti-Blackness"...they operate without any one person actually "doing anything" and it's everywhere...EXCEPT HERE!

**Kim Crayton ~ Antiracist Economist ~ She/Her 🖐️**
@KimCrayton1

As I observe, I expect to see this dynamic shift from Black women to more collaborative engagement or I will, in an effort to minimize harm and to prioritize the most vulnerable, create a separate training for Black women or shut down the training altogether.

11:21AM · Sep 18, 2021 · Twitter for iPhone

**Kim Crayton ~ Antiracist Economist ~ She/Her** 🤲... @KimCrayton1

This is why when I enter spaces, I'm looking for the individuals with the lived experiences as far away from cis, hetero, Christian, white dudes that I can identify and finding ways to center and amplify them

Far too often folx in marginalized communities with power...

Aug 15

EXCLUSIVE: In first interview after Cuomo report and Roberta Kaplan's resignation, #TimesUp President Tina Tchen acknowledges "a blindspot I had" regarding the organization's ties to the powerful & said its conflicts-of-interest policy "isn't sufficient"
19thnews.org/2021/08/times-...

**Kim Crayton ~ Antiracist Economist ~ She/Her** 🤲
@KimCrayton1

and privilege aren't able or willing to see the harm they inflict because it requires them to prioritize the most vulnerable even when doing so doesn't benefit them

This is something I'm ALWAYS examining in my work...how am I able to leverage...

**Kim Crayton ~ Antiracist Economist ~ She/Her** 🤲
@KimCrayton1

the systems, institutions & policies of oppression, discrimination, racism & harm in service to myself and how can I minimize the potential for harming others

If you're not willing or capable of this level of self-reflection & accountability...then you're not doing the work

9:05AM · Aug 15, 2021 · Twitter for iPhone

**Kim Crayton ~ Antiracist Economist ~ She/Her** 🖤
@KimCrayton1

Tech is not neutral nor apolitical AND @Nextdoor has a LONG way to go to ensure that its platform/users prioritize the most vulnerable which INCLUDES addressing issues related to perpetuating racism and discrimination against the unhoused

10:32AM · Nov 9, 2021 · Twitter for iPhone

**Kim Crayton ~ Antiracist Economist ~ She/Her** 🌀... @KimCrayton1
So there's something I want to make clear since several folx have brought it up since sharing my book's cover...the fact that @anildash is providing the book's foreword

If y'all think that building a supremacy, coercion, discrimination, and exploitation FREE future means...

> Replied to you

After the whole Glitch thing, a year or two back.., yeah.

You replied

After the whole Glitch thing, a year or two back.., yeah.

Yep. It was 2 years ago and he corrected what I called out. We all have a lot to learn on this journey and I don't hold folx to a standard that I wouldn't be held to...would you?

**Kim Crayton ~ Antiracist Economist ~ She/Her** 🌀 🤍
@KimCrayton1

I'm not looking for perfect because it just doesn't exist...but I do expect you and others to prioritize the most vulnerable, own your mistakes and make amends when you cause harm

I get that some don't understand or like my choice and I'm fine with that

**Kim Crayton ~ Antiracist Economist ~ She/Her** 🖤🤍
@KimCrayton1

I too found "bootlickers" problematic due to its usage in the Black community and why white folx should've stayed quiet

A "revolution" that DOES NOT seek to identify and prioritize the most vulnerable will target the very individuals least able to shield themselves from harm

Jun 3

And have the nerve to be agreeing with      calling us bootlickers.

So what makes us bootlickers? We ain't liberal leftist enough for you? We don't Tweet enough about it?

What is it. WHAT IS IT.

2:48PM · Jun 3, 2021 · Twitter for iPhone

**Kim Crayton ~ Antiracist Economist ~ She/Her** 🌍... @KimCrayton1
My truth...

After today's exchange, I can admit that there's more I need to understand regarding gender AND I can honestly say that I do not feel any more informed about how to seek the opinions of "women" related to completing my pleasure survey

 **Kim Crayton ~ Antiracist Economist ~ She/Her** 🌍... @KimCrayton1
Yes, I understand that gender is not a binary but because this is not my lived experience, I'm challenged with how to language my need in order to get to the folx who's opinions matter for this project

 **Kim Crayton ~ Antiracist Economist ~ She/Her** 🌍... @KimCrayton1
What I know as a Black woman is that my pleasure has always been in service to or the responsibility of someone else, which means that I've rarely thought about my pleasure without some external condition and with various degrees of guilt and shame...

 **Kim Crayton ~ Antiracist Economist ~ She/Her** 🌍... @KimCrayton1
and I'd like to know what pleasures other women enjoy

Unfortunately, in my effort to be "inclusive", by adding "non-binary", I fact have caused harm AND I can admit that I'm not at all clear how to not replicate such harm in the future

 **Kim Crayton ~ Antiracist Economist ~ She/Her** 🌍... @KimCrayton1
So I'm writing this not as an excuse or to avoid accountability but to demonstrate and model that making mistakes, when we're attempting to create an experience that was never meant to exist, particularly within systems, institutions, and policies...

 **Kim Crayton ~ Antiracist Economist ~ She/Her** 🌍
@KimCrayton1

of supremacy, oppression, and discrimination, will happen but that shouldn't stop us from learning newer, more nuanced ways to prioritize the most vulnerable

1:49PM · Oct 16, 2021 · Twitter for iPhone

**Kim Crayton ~ Antiracist Economist ~ She/Her** ... @KimCrayton1
Who's ready to have some serious conversation related to
#ProfitWithoutOppression because this didn't have to happen AND
this response is just another way we JUSTIFY debating the humanity
of those we see as "other"

>  Nov 6
>
> The response to United Airlines killing a disabled person, by
> damaging her wheelchair and forcing her to sit in a painful metal
> replacement for hours should not be WHEELCHAIRS DON'T
> BELONG ON AIRPLANES.
>
> Engracia was a human being. She was murdered. Have some
> damn respect.

**Kim Crayton ~ Antiracist Economist ~ She/Her** 🖤
@KimCrayton1

This is ALSO why folx in marginalized communities
have to figure out how to come together to
prioritize the most vulnerable

Decreasing the harm inflicted against the most
oppressed, discriminated against, exploited
ensures that we ALL benefit

2:05PM · Nov 7, 2021 · Twitter for iPhone

**Kim Crayton ~ Antiracist Economist ~ She/Her** 🌀
@KimCrayton1

As Black folx embrace the prioritization and maintenance of self-care, its the mandate of mental health practitioners and researchers to prioritize the most vulnerable by challenging their own internalized white supremacy and ante-Blackness or cause harm

3:18PM · Jan 19, 2021 · Twitter for iPhone

**Kim Crayton ~ Antiracist Economist ~ She/Her** 🌀
@KimCrayton1

This is how an individuals belief/opinion has the potential to cause harm

This is rooted in privilege & the ability to leverage the systems, institutions & policies of oppression & discrimination

This is why revolutions that don't prioritize the most vulnerable are problematic

Replying to @KimCrayton1

I don't know what your relationship to Capital is, but I will go to my grave encouraging workers to abolish, rather than flee, oppressive institutions. One great thing about staying at a hateful job, aside from the money, is that it takes a job away from reactionary scabs.

4:20 PM · 6/1/21 · Twitter for Android

2:29PM · Jun 1, 2021 · Twitter for iPhone

**Kim Crayton ~ Antiracist Economist ~ She/Her** 🌑 🐚
@KimCrayton1

"Empathy" is an ex why, if we seek 2 minimize harm & prioritize the most vulnerable, it's important 2 factor in who has had the privilege AND power to develop language

It's IMPOSSIBLE for anyone 2 truly "understand" or experience the "feelings" of others

Seek compassion instead

> 🔖 Save word
>
> ny
>
> hē
>
> em·pa·thy | \ ˈem-pə-thē 🔊 \
>
> **Definition of _empathy_**
>
> 1   : the action of understanding, being aware of, being sensitive to, and vicariously experiencing the feelings, thoughts, and experience of another of either the past or present without having the feelings, thoughts, and
>
> ity to identify with or understand an‹
> ‹ or feelings: synonym: pity.
>
> 🔊 kəm-pãsh'ən
>
> noun
>
> ‹bution of one's own feelings to an ‹
>
> 1. Deep awareness of the suffering of another accompanied by the wish to relieve it. synonym: pity.
>
> ‹lectual identification of the thoughts of another person
>
> 2. Literally, a suffering with another; hence, a feeling of sorrow or pity excited by the sufferings or misfortunes of another; sympathy; commiseration; pity.
>
> Heritage® Dictionary of the English Langu
>
> 3. [Twice used in the plural in the authorized version of the Bible.

2:11PM · Jan 28, 2022 · Twitter for iPhone

**Kim Crayton ~ Antiracist Economist ~ She/Her**
@KimCrayton1

4. Prioritize the Most Vulnerable

This one is easy...

I will NEVER enable whiteness, particularly white women, in harming Black women...PERIOD

I will ALWAYS prioritize my BLACKNESS...PERIOD

I will protect myself and my work because mediocre and unremarkable are NOT my default

9:18AM · Mar 28, 2021 · Twitter Web App

69

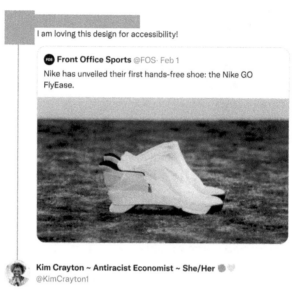

I am loving this design for accessibility!

**Front Office Sports** @FOS· Feb 1

Nike has unveiled their first hands-free shoe: the Nike GO FlyEase.

**Kim Crayton ~ Antiracist Economist ~ She/Her**
@KimCrayton1

This is why INCLUSION matters and why we must prioritize the most vulnerable

As someone who doesn't have accessibility needs related to putting on my shoes, I saw form over function, whereas someone with an accessibility lived experience, saw function over form

Feb 1

I am loving this design for accessibility!

1:34PM · Feb 1, 2021 · Twitter for iPhone

**Kim Crayton ~ Antiracist Economist ~ She/Her**
@KimCrayton1

Black women are the moral compass of this country AND anything that you can think of that makes you too afraid to speak up; to prioritize the most vulnerable...just know that our experience IS worse AND yet we still do it

Mar 1

To think these white supremacists are the ones who go on & on about "cancel culture" my lord. We dared write a peer reviewed paper to get our voices heard & WTF did they unleash on us? They fire me & thats not enough. Gaslighting, lying, unleashing harassers & stalkers who...

8:44PM · Mar 1, 2021 · Twitter for iPhone

# Rules of Engagement

As we advocate for inclusion, equity, and diversity, many are realizing that activating an effective and efficient strategy is far more complex and cumbersome of a prospect than merely having an intention. People are messy and when your goal is to establish welcoming and psychological safety, that mess can appear to be never-ending. Unfortunately, it's the inherently complex nature of the work that causes many to tap out; to throw up their hands and declare the impossible nature of such endeavors. This is a mistake because falure is not an option in an environment that demands, and let's be honest requires, diversity as a fundamental function of success. The alternative, to ignore the lived experiences of the majority of the workforce, is to set out on a course that will inevitably result in harming all stakeholder interest. How do you arm your organization with the processes, policies, and procedures that are rooted in minimizing harm? You build community and develop strategy around The Rules of Engagement. Having a clearly defined yet malleable set of conditions on which all stakeholders can use to further the mission and goals of the organization helps to ensure that at a bare minimum, folx have guidelines for honoring the lived experiences outside of their own.

**Kim Crayton ~ Antiracist Economist ~ She/Her** 🌎... @KimCrayton1
Due to my own curious nature and love of history, I've known about India's caste systems, institutions, and policies for awhile, so the current challenges that are being reported and shared related to caste discrimination in tech, isn't surprising

**Kim Crayton ~ Antiracist Economist ~ She/Her** 🌎... @KimCrayton1
I actually see it as an opportunity to challenge and test my own world view and ongoing #ProfitWithoutOppression research which seeks to establish a supremacy, coercion, discrimination, and exploitation FREE future by questioning how this and other topics, that sit...

**Kim Crayton ~ Antiracist Economist ~ She/Her** 🌎... @KimCrayton1
outside of my personal lived experience, can be addressed in ways that align with the Guiding Principles (PWO-GP)...

PROFIT WITHOUT OPPRESSION
# Guiding Principles:

Tech is Not Neutral, Nor is it Apolitical

Intention without Strategy is Chaos

Lack of Inclusion is a Risk/Crisis Management Issue

Prioritize the Most Vulnerable

@KimCrayton1

**Kim Crayton ~ Antiracist Economist ~ She/Her** 🌎... @KimCrayton1
and what I keep coming back to are the reasons why I developed the Rules of Engagement because any path towards a supremacy, coercion, discrimination, and exploitation FREE future will require that we all focus our attention on minimizing harm but how do we accomplish this

 **Kim Crayton ~ Antiracist Economist ~ She/Her** 🤎... @KimCrayton1
Let me now walk you through this "imperfect" strategy

"Imperfect" not because it's flawed but because, it's human-focused, and I haven't discovered a way to eliminate harm, particularly to the most vulnerable in our efforts to improve everyone's overall lived experiences

 **Kim Crayton ~ Antiracist Economist ~ She/Her** 🤎... @KimCrayton1
Drawing on the PWO-GP, when we can acknowledge that being "apolitical" isn't possible, we then understand the need to ensure that "debates" related to someone's humanity or right to exist, are nonstarters

Such conversations are not only harmful but are indeed POLITICAL

**Kim Crayton ~ Antiracist Economist ~ She/Her** 🌎... @KimCrayton1
When all can acknowledge the harm inflicted when "identity related debates" are permeated and can agree that this behavior is off limits, then we can move forward with shared language, purpose, and strategy

This is where we prioritize LISTENING to UNDERSTAND and NOT to "debate"

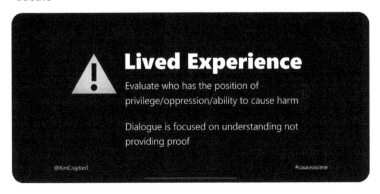

**Kim Crayton ~ Antiracist Economist ~ She/Her** 🌎... @KimCrayton1
Once we've gained some understanding, we're now capable of engaging each other to find commonalities to leverage for welcoming and psychological safety, while respecting the boundaries of our collective differences

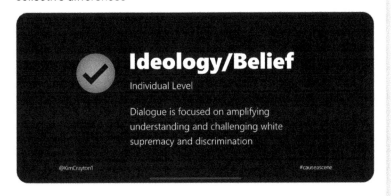

**Kim Crayton ~ Antiracist Economist ~ She/Her** ... @KimCrayton1
This is the challenging but necessary work that must be done in order for tech, as an industry, to shift to a culture that seeks success, while minimizing harm to ALL stakeholders: those who work for, partner with, buy from, are impact by you, and invest in us

 **Kim Crayton ~ Antiracist Economist ~ She/Her** ... @KimCrayton1
As an outsider to these conversations, I'm neither naïve or hold any belief that the suggested path forward, for any marginalized and vulnerable community, will be an easy one but I also know that, BY DESIGN, repeating old patterns hasn't work and that the only way out is through

 **Kim Crayton ~ Antiracist Economist ~ She/Her**
@KimCrayton1

Let me close by reminding you that we get there together or not at all because systems, institutions, and policies DESIGNED to exclude and harm rely on "others" to maintain divisions among ourselves, this is why "individualism" has been such an effective and efficient strategy

7:24AM · Jun 8, 2022 · Twitter for iPhone

**Kim Crayton ~ Antiracist Economist ~ She/Her** 🙏
@KimCrayton1

Rules of engagement for new followers:

~ All whiteness is racist by design

~ Which means that it can't be trusted by default

~ You're not my "ally" & no we're not on the same side

~ This is not a democracy, I don't care about your opinions

#causeascene

5:49PM · Aug 14, 2019 · Twitter for iPhone

**Kim Crayton ~ Antiracist Economist ~ She/Her** 🙏
@KimCrayton1

I find all of this so fascinating

The rules of engagement for white folx ALWAYS has interesting loopholes and hidden clauses which are used to leverage white supremacist systems in your favor

4:31PM · Feb 29, 2020 · Twitter for iPhone

77

**Kim Crayton ~ Antiracist Economist ~ She/Her** ⬤
@KimCrayton1

This is an example of why I do not advocate "debating" these issues

Debates begin with individuals who agree on rules of engagement

These are not debates because

YOUR BELIEFS != MY RIGHT TO EXIST

THERE'S JUST NO COMMON GROUND TO BEGIN A "DISCUSSION"

#causeascene

> Oct 29
>
> The right: *uses government to take away my basic human rights and dignity because I'm trans*
>
> Me: *any kind of reaction at all*
>
> The right: "Identity politics!"

7:21PM · Oct 29, 2018 · Twitter for iPhone

**Kim Crayton ~ Antiracist Economist ~ She/Her** 🌑... @KimCrayton1
As someone who spends most of my time thinking about and
experimenting with the ideas of a supremacy, coercion,
discrimination, and exploitation FREE future, I force myself to
evaluate subject matter from varies angles, perspectives, and levels
of comfort, many which require...

**Kim Crayton ~ Antiracist Economist ~ She/Her** 🌑... @KimCrayton1
me to decenter myself and yield my needs/wants in
support/protection to those who're more vulnerable than I am

Being able, as a researcher, to set aside my own desires, in a world
designed for us to disregard solidarity with "others" in service to...

**Kim Crayton ~ Antiracist Economist ~ She/Her** 🌑... @KimCrayton1
elevating "individualism" or ones affinity group, often feels like a fish
fighting against water; pretty fuckin unnatural, but it's been through
developing a practice of observation and self- reflection that I'm able
to recognize and acknowledge my personal bias and their...

**Kim Crayton ~ Antiracist Economist ~ She/Her** 🌑... @KimCrayton1
impact on my beliefs and decisions that enabled me to develop the
#ProfitWithoutOppression Guiding Principles and the...

PROFIT WITHOUT OPPRESSION
## Guiding Principles:

Tech is Not Neutral, Nor is it Apolitical

Intention without Strategy is Chaos

Lack of Inclusion is a Risk/Crisis Management Issue

Prioritize the Most Vulnerable

@KimCrayton1

**Kim Crayton ~ Antiracist Economist ~ She/Her** 🖐️ 🌾
@KimCrayton1

"Rules of Engagement" because without adopting adequate tools and strategies that help counter the intended impact that enable systems, institutions, and policies, designed to privilege the few while excluding and harming the many, we find ourselves...

**Kim Crayton ~ Antiracist Economist ~ She/Her** 🖐️ 🌾
@KimCrayton1

leveraging and aiming those same mechanisms of oppression and violence which target us towards "others"

Life is messy and complex and, unfortunately, it is our lack of experience with navigating the "messy and complex", which is also by design, that causes us to see enemies...

**Kim Crayton ~ Antiracist Economist ~ She/Her** 🖤
@KimCrayton1

with those we should be seeking community; with those whose lived experiences have positioned them to be our guides through the worse of who we can be to our collective liberation

This world I seek to experience; this world where supremacy over "others" by denying...

**Kim Crayton ~ Antiracist Economist ~ She/Her** 🖤
@KimCrayton1

their "right" to live their truth is not required for me to exist in peace; to thrive; to evolve into my highest self

I also know that this is not my dream alone

There are many who would choose this path forward if only they knew how; if only they could orient their...

**Kim Crayton ~ Antiracist Economist ~ She/Her** 🖤
@KimCrayton1

personal perspectives to one which sees differences as something to embrace and celebrate rather than something to control/dominate; to one which sees power as something to be shared rather than exploited; to one which sees harmony as a worthy endeavor rather than weakness

**Kim Crayton ~ Antiracist Economist ~ She/Her**
@KimCrayton1

This world I seek to experience, which challenges me daily by forcing me to evaluate my relationship with "we" rather than "I", is founded on the fundamental understanding, history is full of examples, that we get there together or not at all

7:13AM · Jul 5, 2022 · Twitter Web App

**Kim Crayton ~ Antiracist Economist ~ She/Her** ... @KimCrayton1
THIS SPEAKS TO THE FLAW IN YOUR ARGUMENT

Those who FEEL victimized and those who ARE victimized should not be afforded the same treatment

Think about what that would look like in an emergency room setting

Total chaos

#causeascene

**Kim Crayton ~ Antiracist Economist ~ She/Her**
@KimCrayton1

This is why I developed hierarchical rules of engagement, which support:

~ Prioritize the Most Vulnerable

~ Intention Without Strategy Is Chaos

Also, where is your plan of action

You've said a lot and have yet to lay out a STRATEGY for accomplishing any of it

#causeascene

## Rules of Engagement [Bases on Whose Needs & Safety Are Prioritized]

### Questioning Humanity/Right to Exist [Red]
- Community Level

### Lived Experience [Yellow]
- Evaluate who has the position of privilege/oppression/ability to cause harm
- Dialogue is focused on understanding not providing proof

### Ideology/Belief [Green]
- Individual Level
- Dialogue is focused on amplifying understanding and challenging white supremacy and discrimination

7:36AM · May 6, 2019 · Twitter Web Client

**Kim Crayton ~ Antiracist Economist ~ She/Her** 🤲... @KimCrayton1

"In order to arrive at a mutually harmonious and correct conclusion, the result of a logical argument, we must have a premise or point of beginning upon which we can all agree." ~ Charles Fillmore

This is why the adoption of the Guiding Principles is key...

### individualism
ĭn″də-vĭj′oō-ə-lĭz″əm

noun

1. Belief in the primary importance of the individual and in the virtues of self-reliance and personal independence.

2. Acts or an act based on this belief.

3. A doctrine advocating freedom from government regulation in the pursuit of a person's economic goals.

The American Heritage® Dictionary of the English Language, 5th

### community
kə-myoō′nĭ-tē

noun

1. A group of people living in the same locality and under the same government.

2. The district or locality in which such a group lives.

3. A group of people having common interests.

The American Heritage® Dictionary of the English Language, 5th Edition

noun

1. A room or enclosure with acoustically reflective walls used in broadcasting and recording to produce echoes or similar sound effects.

2. A room with walls that resonate sound, producing audible echoes; it is used especially to create special sound effects in recording music.

3. A room or other enclosed space that is highly conducive to the production of echoes, particularly one that has been designed and built for this purpose.

PROFIT WITHOUT OPPRESSION

### Guiding Principles:

Tech is Not Neutral, Nor is it Apolitical

Intention without Strategy is Chaos

Lack of Inclusion is a Risk/Crisis Management Issue

Prioritize the Most Vulnerable

**Kim Crayton ~ Antiracist Economist ~ She/Her** 🙏... @KimCrayton1
I'm willing to discuss anything as long as there's common ground
rooted in equity

I refuse to engage in ANY activity [conversation/new client/project]
that at the very least, don't have the Guiding Principles as an agreed
upon starting point

Anything less is a distraction

**Kim Crayton ~ Antiracist Economist ~ She/Her** 🙏
@KimCrayton1

Folx often rebut, when you refuse to
engage/debate, that they've "won" and/or that
you're scared...for me, neither is true nor does it
matter because I have agency over where I place
my attention and resources

Also, even "debates" begin with agreed upon rules
of engagement

---

# debate

 dĭ-bāt′

intransitive verb

1. To consider something; deliberate.

2. To engage in argument by discussing opposing
   points.

3. To engage in a formal discussion or argument.
   synonym: discuss.

The American Heritage® Dictionary of the English Language, 5th
Edition.

5:55AM · Nov 13, 2021 · Twitter for iPhone

**Kim Crayton ~ Antiracist Economist ~ She/Her** 🧡🧡
@KimCrayton1

This is what it looks like when whiteness has learned to move around the world as if they own the space

Unfortunately, wild animals haven't had the pleasure of being indoctrinated into respecting rules of engagement

Also, moving back decreases animal's spaces

#causeascene

**CBS Evening News** @CBSEveningNews· Mar 12

Woman injured by jaguar at Arizona zoo: "I was in the wrong for leaning over the barrier, but I do think that maybe the zoo should look into moving their fence back."

9:10AM · Mar 12, 2019 · Twitter for iPhone

# Questioning Humanity and the Right to Exist

In our efforts to establish welcoming and psychological safety, we will encounter folx whose lived experiences and self-identities we may be unfamiliar and even uncomfortable with. It is during these moments when what we "know to be true" about the world is challenged, when our curiosity is peaked and our defenses may go up, that we must commit ourselves to minimizing harm. It is when we may be at our most vulnerable that we seek to establish and maintain a practice of never questioning the humanity or the right to exist of others. If it is a supremacy-, coercion-, discrimination-, and exploitation-free future that we seek, we must commit to behaving in ways that, particularly when we believe that our own identity is being challenged, dictate that we aren't operating from a zero-sum game perspective. From a place where "a fight for me has to come at the expense of you." In our efforts to define how we engage with others, at all times, our foundational understanding should be that challenging or defending a position does not require denying another's right to do the same and to do so with dignity.

**Kim Crayton ~ Antiracist Economist ~ She/Her** 🖤🤎
@KimCrayton1

I understand that my "right" to exist; to thrive; to
be FREE, is intimately tied to these same desires
being shared amongst us all

I know that if I don't seek to protect the more
vulnerable, that when they're no longer the targets,
because they are no more, then I'm next

8:13PM · Jul 4, 2022 · Twitter Web App

# Lived Experience

Everyone arrives at each situation with their own unique worldview as a result of our personal lived experiences. There are no two people who engage with their surroundings in the exact same way...not even those among us with identical DNA. So it's never made sense, other than as a tool to leverage the few at the expense of the many, to behave in ways that value a monolithic view. Homogeneity appears to make life easier; makes those who benefit from the status quo feel comfortable. But one's sense of ease and comfort is tenuous because its foundation is like sand; always shifting. It's only when we acknowledge and embrace the role that lived experiences play in shaping our unique perspectives that we can begin to build our lives, our organizations, on solid ground. As with any construction site, the goal is to build on the sturdiest of foundations since the alternatives entail eventual collapse and destruction. Construction companies employ tools, machinery, and equipment that's designed to break through the hardest of substances to anchor their construction on. Not only does doing the hard work of preparing the foundation before erecting the frame pay off in keeping the building intact, it also helps to minimize potential harm by helping builders identify and mitigate any weak points discovered along the way. The same can be said for lived experience. Our ability and willingness to understand the lived experiences of the many aids organizational leaders in identifying and managing foundational points of strength and weakness, which enables them to better leverage knowledge for the development of organizational outcomes and an informed risk-management strategy.

**Kim Crayton ~ Antiracist Economist ~ She/Her** 
@KimCrayton1

In the information economy, business leaders MUST begin to hire for lived experiences [diversity i.e. recruitment] and [inclusion i.e. retention] to compete

More than ever before, lack of inclusion is a risk, and increasingly a crisis, management issue

> ████████████ Jul 23
> It's occurring to me that I have a unicorn set of skills for an engineer: principal level, standards experience, distributed services experience at extreme scale (npm), enterprise experience, startup experience, multilingual, community organizer, speaker, teacher, woman, black.

9:40PM · Jul 23, 2020 · Twitter for iPhone

"When you cannot talk about race, you exclude my lived experience." -- @KimCrayton1

10:56AM · Jun 27, 2020 · Twitter Web App

"Privilege" is about access.
"Underrepresented" is about numbers.
"Diversity" is about variety.
"Inclusion" is about lived experience.

@KimCrayton1 on the #BIPOCinTech live (virtual)
stage beginning with FACTS.

11:10AM · Sep 15, 2021 · Twitter Web App

**Kim Crayton ~ Antiracist Economist ~ She/Her** 🖤 🤎
@KimCrayton1

Due to my understanding of whiteness, if your lived experience doesn't also intersect w at least one marginalized or vulnerable community, I do NOT trust your identity as liberal/progressive & even then there MUST be a record of demonstrated, consistent de-centering of whiteness

6:43AM · Oct 14, 2021 · Twitter for iPhone

**Kim Crayton ~ Antiracist Economist ~ She/Her** 🖤 🤎
@KimCrayton1

High Tweet 2

Individualism/exceptionalism doesn't make space for an undivided Universe; a lived experience that operates from an understanding that, we're unique expressions of the same Universal truth...ENERGY

It's only our manifested world that creates the illusion of division

3:53PM · Jun 7, 2022 · Twitter for iPhone

# Ideology / Belief

Our "beliefs" can be tricky because so often, if we take time to reflect and self-evaluate, we discover that what we "believe" isn't the result of our personal discovery but rather the "beliefs" adopted for our "in- group;" those individuals we most iden-tify with. Many will spend their entire lives parroting, without much thought, these "beliefs" as their own. It's usually not until we find ourselves in a situation where our "beliefs" cause harm, both intended and unintended, that we take the time to evalu-ate these "beliefs" against what's in the best interest of ourselves and those we care about, that we begin to question their truth and value. We base our decisions and actions on our "beliefs," and we can only assess the impact of our "beliefs" on how well they serve us and our willingness to accept responsibility for our actions through our lived experiences. When left unexam-ined, we often face the consequences, particularly for the most powerful and privileged, for which we don't fully understand. Taking time to dissect our "beliefs" and their potential impact on ourselves and others is a healthy step in building community. It enables us to enter spaces as the best reflection of ourselves while holding space for others. It allows us to better understand our potential points of failure and extend grace to others. It helps us to operate with the knowledge that establishing an organizational culture of welcoming and psychological safety isn't about the false narrative of neutrality or being "apolitical" or assimilation but instead finding ways to build community through diversity.

**Kim Crayton ~ Antiracist Economist ~ She/Her** 🖤
@KimCrayton1

So many folx, particularly those in positions of power and privilege, exist in binaries...binaries cause so much harm

This is my BIGGEST issue with folx who think they have "liberal" or "progressive" ideology

They care more about the "revolution" than being revolutionary

8:06AM · Sep 11, 2021 · Twitter for iPhone

An 18 year-old from a town with a Black population less than 1% travels hours to Buffalo to kill Black people because he hears they are "replacing" Caucasians. Who filled his head with this poison? We must stop Big Tech from propagating Big Lies that lead to carnage.

Republicans. It was Republicans.

Hey race-baiting leftists, I am much more opposed to liberal white "replacements" coming to Texas & perfectly happy to have "brown" people you all like to endanger for your political games legally come! Tell you what, how about you leave pushing great replacement theory claiming white people are intentionally being replaced by migrants

By Christopher Eberhart For Dailymail.Com
20 36 EDT 18 Sep 2021 , updated 21 41 EDT 18 Sep 2021

replacement theory

By Greg Sargent
Columnist + Follow

April 6, 2022 at 11:31 a.m. EDT

I have spoken to white a few Democrats whose views are only slightly less extreme.

 **Kim Crayton ~ Antiracist Economist ~ She/Her** ●
@KimCrayton1

When are we gonna stop "segregating" proponents of white supremacy & anti-Blackness to party affiliation/ideology

Most white folx will ALWAYS prioritize whiteness because not doing so would NOT be in their best interest

Whiteness is under attack == white folx are under attack

May 16

I have spoken to white a few Democrats whose views are only slightly less extreme.

8:47PM · May 16, 2022 · Twitter for iPhone

**Kim Crayton ~ Antiracist Economist ~ She/Her**
@KimCrayton1

White supremacy is an ideology

Racism is a strategy that promotes the ideology of white supremacy

Racist are those individuals who benefit from the ideology of white supremacy, regardless of active/willing or passive/unwilling participation

#causeascene

**CBS Mornings** @CBSMornings· Aug 12

Two years ago today, #Charlottesville, Virginia became a flashpoint for America's racial tension, with violent clashes between white supremacists & counter-protesters.

@AmericanU's @DrIbram leads an open & honest conversation about race with a group of people who were there.

RACIAL TENSIONS IN AMERICA
CHARLOTTESVILLE RESIDENTS DISCUSS RACE 2 YEARS AFTER DEADLY RIOT

3:56PM · Aug 12, 2019 · Twitter Web App

# The Future Is Free.

The belief that "what is," is, and that "what is" can't change governs many aspects of our daily life. This understanding of the world and how we experience it results from intentional strategy. The exclusion, the obstacles, and the violence didn't just happen. One such strategy, The Powell Memo (see Appendix 1), first sparked the idea that if folx used strategy to privilege the few at the expense of the many, then I could develop a strategy to have the lived experience I'd like to have and share that with others. It was the drive to develop strategy that included rather than excluded. That amplified rather than silenced. That was hopeful instead of violent and led to the creation of the Guiding Principles, which led to The Rules of Engagement, which led to the creation of the Profit Without Oppression economic theory, which led to focusing solely on building a practice and body of work that is supremacy-, coercion-, discrimination-, and exploitation-FREE.

# Knowledge Is Power, and Ignorance Is No longer An Excuse for Causing Harm.

In the information age, remaining ignorant of one's impact on others is a choice that has always served the goals of the powerful and privileged. When we thought that all of the world's knowledge was held in sets of encyclopedias and other reference materials on shelves in quiet buildings, ignorance was an easier state of being to nurture and manage, but no longer. Except for increasingly smaller parts of society, most folx can now access information from their pockets, purses, and wrists. With the increased information access comes an increasing intolerance for ignorance to be used as an excuse for escaping being accountable for one's actions. When you can now learn about the most random subject matter, remaining oblivious to historical efforts to enshrine exclusion and violence into systems, institutions, and policies is a choice that no longer frees you to behave in ways that cause harm. Ignorance may be bliss, but escaping accountability is now harder than ever. Although this has only been the case for the privileged few, ignorance is no longer liability-free. Information is the only path to knowledge, which is the only path to wisdom.

**Kim Crayton ~ Antiracist Economist ~ She/Her** 🌐
@KimCrayton1

Our lack of historical acumen has been a deliberate and successful strategy

Ignorance, willful or otherwise, is the breeding ground for ideology/beliefs that are rooted in the justification for chaos, destruction, and the harming of others

Jan 3

Right wing anti-communist/anti-socialism/anti-marxist talking points are just neo-nazi propaganda rebranded for better optics.

12:49PM · Jan 3, 2021 · Twitter for iPhone

**Kim Crayton ~ Antiracist Economist ~ She/Her** 🖤
@KimCrayton1

"Misogyny is more than just a construct and systemic form of oppression, it is a choice, it is an ideology people still feel comfortable ascribing to, supporting and perpetuating because it benefits them on one level or another. "

#causeascene

2:03PM · Mar 30, 2019 · Buffer

https://www.greaterthancode.com/cause-a-scene

# Black Women Are the Moral Compass.

Due to the global acceptance and adoption of white supremacy, anti-Blackness, and patriarchal dominance, Black women uniquely sit at the intersection of exclusion and violence in ways that white women [patriarchy] and Black men [racism] don't. This intersectional point means that the lived experiences of Black women make them experts in navigating both gender and race. Black women, whose only accepted function in society has been to serve others, who have historically been the world's caregivers, do so while simultaneously having to manage their role as the connecting thread for future generations of Black folx. It is also Black women who have been the targets of gender and racialized harm who are best equipped to develop counter-strategy.

**Kim Crayton ~ Antiracist Economist ~ She/Her**
@KimCrayton1

It's not hyperbole for me to say that Black women are the moral compass and that our COLLECTIVE liberation is through us

Black women EVERYWHERE are targets of harm at disproportionate rates, so of course we're better positioned to create solutions

businessinsider.com/black-women-bu…

**Black-owned businesses took a pandemic hit, but they're doing better than ever now — largely because of Black women**

Jason Lalljee  3 min read

- The number of Black-owned firms shrank at the start of the pandemic, but is now higher than before.

- Black women are creating more businesses than their female counterparts in any other demographic.

- In fact, women of color have been fueling the creation of a record

more Black women are electing to become CEOs of their own companies rather than waiting for their intelligence and skills to be recognized at their current firms," Melissa Bradley, the founder of 1863 Ventures, an agency for Black and brown entrepreneurs, told Insider.

After all, Black women are paid less than any other demographic group and overrepresented in low-paying jobs, so pursuing their own business venture is a way to gain more control over their work lives. Black women's entrepreneurship gains in particular align with their exodus from the workforce as millions of women have left due to a lack of childcare, adequate pay,

5:40AM · Feb 8, 2022 · Twitter for iPhone

# Find the Darkest Women, Trans, and Non-Binary Folx In Any Community for Practical Solutions to Many of Our Problems.

As previously stated, Black women, and I'll add trans and non-binary folx, find themselves uniquely equipped to navigate the complex nature of sexism and racism. Still, due to white supremacy and anti-Blackness, the darkest Black folx experience the most harm inflicted at this intersection. Therefore it makes sense to seek out the expertise of these most vulnerable folx for solutions while always compensating them equitably for the trauma that they will inevitably experience doing so because this work, for these folx, causes them harm.

# We Will All Make Mistakes Because We're Trying to Create an Inclusive Experience that Was Never Meant to Exist.

The work needed to build a supremacy-, coercion-, discrimination-, and exploitation-FREE future won't be easy. There will be obstacles and challenges at every step because this work requires facing off against the status quo; it requires folx to make decisions that prioritize those whom current systems, institutions, and policies have intentionally excluded and targeted for harm. It's counter to everything we've been taught about "success" and belonging. Hell, given the history of the United States, I should be a slave. The fact that I am not is because folx decided to challenge the status quo. It is in the footsteps of those individuals that we continue the journey forward, understanding that this is uncharted territory. There are no roadmaps. Some of us have taken on the responsibility of clearing the way for others to follow, understanding that we will, unfortunately, cause harm along the way. This work requires us to move slowly, being mindful of where we are going while taking deliberate and strategic steps forward. This is why it's important to continually reflect on:

- Was harm caused?
- Who was harmed?
- How were they harmed?
- How do we make amends/make them whole again?

# How To Apologize and Make Amends

We all make mistakes. And as we move forward with building alternatives to systems, institutions, and policies designed to privilege the few at the expense of the many, unfortunately, we will fuck up a lot, but fucking up doesn't have to be game over. Fucking up is often the most effective way to ensure that the resulting harm is not replicated, so I get it. What I don't get is not knowing how to set things right; how few folx know how to repair the damage they cause; have no clue of how to move beyond shame, guilt, and anger. An apology is simply an acknowledgement of harm, a commitment to do better, and an agreed-upon path forward that seeks to make those harmed as whole again as possible.

**Kim Crayton ~ Antiracist Economist ~ She/Her** 🌑
@KimCrayton1

How to Apologize 101:

1. I apologize for causing harm

2. I take responsibility that the harm I caused had the following impact [be SPECIFIC]

3. This is how I plan to make amends [be SPECIFIC]

That's it! Nothing about you, your feelings or your intention

#causeascene

3:21PM · Feb 6, 2020 · Twitter for iPhone

# Commentary

The process I developed as an educator and adopted for this work is "stop doing that;" this is "why you will stop doing that;" "this is what we will do instead." Every day, someone comes to my content at the very beginning of their journey and wants me to explain something repeatedly. As an educator, you understand that at some point, that no longer becomes beneficial, like you just need to keep practicing your ABCs. No, no, no. We need to start creating words. You know your ABCs, you can't do shit with just your ABCs, so this is where we are right now. There are enough folx who understand that the work I did with #causeascene was needed. When the language of welcoming and psychological safety was new for folx, and you needed someone like me, who is also learning the language, but who could also teach along the way and show folx what was going on. Now there are enough folx who understand, particularly given the cultural climate, how these systems, institutions, and policies are designed to harm and so now it's time to move on to do the work of building alternatives. To challenge the idea that exclusion and harm "just happened." No, we're here because of strategy. So when folx think that harm is inevitable, they don't know what can be done, what they can do. So folx get stuck in, specifically white folx, and they see themselves as victims. They then can't/don't do shit, which helps no one. Then there are the folx who see everything but don't understand there is a strategy behind it because every system, institution, and policy cloaks the intentional and strategic nature of white supremacy and anti-Blackness. This is why they don't want you to learn history. For white supremacy to thrive, it requires that those who benefit from its unearned privileges remain strategically ignorant; that your well-being and success comes at the expense of others. That you never learn that the harm that they endure is not a result of personal failing but of targeted exclusion and violence. White supremacy is designed to keep us from seeing the connection. It is designed to keep us from understanding how the success of the few requires the harming of the many. The goal is that you will never see it because then you will realize that "Oh shit, this didn't just come out of nowhere. This is a direct response to that thing we did."

# Case Study: Erin

## How did you meet Kim?

I was introduced to Kim by a project. It was the first project I secured in my new business. I run a marketing and events business called Strat House, and this was my very first client. It was a software client I had done work for in the past, and they reached out to me and said, *"I heard you're starting your own agency; I have a project I would like to bring you on for."* At that time, the project was labeled an untitled DE&I event. They wanted someone who could strategically help support this event and help them think through it and how to produce it. I came on board and started to work with our client team at that technology company.

It became apparent early on that we would need to seek outside counsel to make this event successful, and it was recommended that we initiate a steerco, a steering committee internally. The primary demographic of this event was to be BIPOC community, but also co-conspirators should be an important part of it too. We just knew this was something outside our subject matter of expertise in terms of how to do that and engage everyone in the right way appropriately. So our steering committee was comprised of several BIPOC team members within the organization who put forth a couple of ideas. Kim Crayton was on their list and her name quickly rose to the top. I reached out to Kim via LinkedIn. I explained to her the event background and what we were trying to achieve and asked her if she would be interested in coming on board as our content producer and our host. We gave her ownership over the event trajectory as well as the event itself by really being the persona who helped us bring this event to life and helped us moderate it.

## What was your initial experience with her, the first time you worked together?

After we got through the negotiations and the billing process, it was time for us to hop on our first call. That initial conversation with Kim was a moment that I will never forget. It was two other white women and me (also a white woman). We got on the call with Kim and she was there with her assistant, Lauren. It was one of the most eye-opening experiences I have had in my professional life.

Kim was incredibly well prepared. She had read all the advance details we shared with her, and the first thing she did was obliterate the plan. She said, *"I read through everything, and I think there is a big gap in your strategy."* She essentially identified several flaws in what we put forth, and I was immediately grateful because that was exactly what we had hoped for when we enlisted an expert, someone with the right philosophies and intentions for the event. So immediately, I was delighted, but I was also terrified. I was nervous. I thought I was going to say something wrong. I had already done something wrong in putting together this strategy, and I did feel like I was flying blind—which, if Kim was here would note is an ableist phrase. I am consistently learning from Kim. Let me try that again: I felt as though I did not have the right experience to lead this event. This type of work was something I had never done before. Kim came at us with an intensity, fervor, and bluntness I had rarely experienced. To quote Kim, *"I am coming at you at a 10 because any other Black person in this position would come at you at a two. I'm having the voice that should be and is deserved to be heard, and I am doing so in this way because most of the community wouldn't come at you at the appropriate level. They would come at you at a two, and so I do this on behalf of the community so that others don't have to."* The conversation continued and one of things Kim was rightfully questioning in our strategy was why would you combine the BIPOC community together with the non-BIPOC community in an event if you're trying to create a welcoming and psychologically safe place? Why would you want to talk about co-conspiratorship with a blended audience? That should be a separate workstream. Kim quickly made us realize if we want to create a psychologically safe place for the BIPOC community that these needed to be two separate events, and she was absolutely correct. When she started to go into the rationale behind our idea, she started to talk about some of the principles that I know will be in the book, like the tendencies that white folks have to center themselves in these conversations and their inability to manage their own feelings. As she is discussing these principles, I find that I am doing exactly what she said shouldn't be done because it gets in the way of the work. Immediately in my head I'm becoming very defensive, I am centering my emotions, I feel caught off guard, and I am feeling incredibly nervous. I was thinking about all this rationale, and I felt this need to defend the strategy. It was incredibly eye-opening to understand that these inherent reactions are problematic. It was very apparent from this first conversation that I could learn so much professionally and personally from Kim. And it was even more apparent that she was the right person to bring on to help shape these events. I don't think I ever got off a conference call with my jaw on my floor. I was completely shocked by what had just happened, but it was also invigorated and I felt challenged in a good way. I felt wowed. I had so much to learn, and I felt very excited I had the opportunity to work with someone who could teach me.

## What are the most profound things you learned while working with Kim?

One of the most profound things I have learned by working with Kim is the necessity of being uncomfortable in this work, that there is no convenience, that if you're doing it correctly, then the work is never-ending. I think for someone like myself and most business leaders, the fact that there is an elusive outcome is very daunting. I think because of that, folks tire and the systems, institutions, and policies that currently impede progress and social change remain because folx like to check boxes. They like to complete the task. They like to forecast, have a three-, six-, and nine-month plan. This work is never done because of its systemic nature. I think the understanding of just how deeply-rooted and ingrained oppression is has been one of the most profound things I've come to understand in my life.

To give a small example of one of the things Kim did early on in our relationship: I tend to use the words "guys" when I reference a group of folks, like *"Hey guys,"* or *"You guys will line up for rehearsal over here."* She corrected me and said *"Choosing a familiar reference that does not include gender would be the right way to go, so I use the word folx."* So for an entire year in working together to plan that first event, every time I said the word guys she would correct me. Every single time. I eventually began

113

correcting myself, and then I found myself correcting others. I still find myself slipping. The work is never done.

More recently, Kim and I were working together in a production document for our upcoming podcast. We wanted to talk about the notion of white folx having a Black friend and wearing that as a badge of honor. I was typing our notes, and I wrote the word "black" and it was not capitalized. Kim said *"You need to capitalize Black,"* and I said *"Yes, thank you,"* and I corrected it on screen. Only a moment later, I did it again in the next sentence. Kim corrected me again. As I fixed my second error, I was thinking in my head *"Kim, I didn't mean anything by it. I am just typing quickly because I want to get all of these good ideas down."* Right there in that moment I was potentially causing harm but immediately my defense mechanisms tuned up. My emotions were getting the best of me and I was centering myself, taking away from the important work. That's just how pervasive and systemic this all is.

I share these examples to highlight that antiracism is a consistent daily practice like Kim likes to say, and for you to understand it is going to be uncomfortable, it is going to be challenging. That is one of the most profound things I've learned from Kim.

I think the other thing that is deeply profound is understanding the toll, dedication, and commitment it takes on Kim's part to be in this position and to do that correcting. I think it was eye-opening because unfortunately, white folx turn to Black folx in my observation—sometimes in a well-intentioned way but causing harm — because they are interested or expecting a level of education so that they can behave as they should. That is not the job of the Black community, and that has been incredibly eye-opening. Kim, however, has taken that job on. She has committed herself to do that work. For me, it has been mindblowing to witness how taxing and tiring that is. I am just incredibly in awe of how Kim can renew herself daily after having to be the one who points out these opportunities to learn and be better.

## How did the team respond to the things she was saying, and how did Kim come off?

I thought that despite the initial shock and awe of the first conversation, the team met Kim with open arms. It was quickly apparent we needed to elevate the conversation that we were having with Kim to the stakeholder of the company who was a C-level executive and the executive sponsor of the event. Once we had a chance to connect them directly, they were able to have a candid conversation about what the event should be and how the event strategy by the time it landed with Kim had gone a bit sideways. I think what was so interesting about that was it became proof of why events like this need to exist. It was also proof that systems, institutions, and policies that Kim is always looking to change and advance are currently designed as Kim has described. They are made for chaos and destruction, and that's what happens in any organization unfortunately when folx go to work on a plan. Often the intention gets lost and harm usually ensues. The fact that we were able to get Kim in the right room to have the conversation with the executive sponsor and the stakeholder got everyone fully on board with Kim and also with her as the face and voice of the event. Her no-holds-barred commentary was welcomed and appreciated, and she was really viewed as a collaborator even as it related to developing the event's code of conduct and helping us to delicately navigate the co-conspirator track.

## How necessary do you think this level of honesty is for this level of organization and business?

I think it's critical, and I think like anything, the most critical work is the hardest. I also think that unfortunately, right now folks view it as ancillary or nice to have. By checking the box thing, we want to show we have ERGs (employee resource groups). We want to show we are doing the right thing. We want to show that we are compliant. I think what is interesting about Kim's work is that the honesty forces us to have these conversations quicker. I also believe honesty allows folks to understand the harm quickly. There is no sugarcoating it. It's almost like you cannot un-see or un-hear it once you hear Kim speak, so I think it's a forcing function. At that point, if you hear Kim speak and you hear what she says and you don't recognize the truth in what she is saying, you are choosing to ignore it. You're making a conscious choice, and at that point, you are culpable. So I think it is critical.

## Why do you believe this work is exhausting?

I get to watch a lot of Kim's work play out on Twitter. Once Kim sees violation or harm, she is compelled. She cannot look the other way because of her commitment and because of her vision of what can be possible. She has this responsibility that she certainly owns, and it requires that when she sees harm or an opportunity to educate someone, she takes it. This comes with a tremendous amount of backlash because again, pointing back to one of her principles, folks immediately center themselves in conversations that are not designed for them, that they should not be a part of, and they prioritize their feelings instead of prioritizing the most vulnerable. There is just this entire faction of folx who for whatever motivation get involved, and so I see this play out on the world stage. I see it play out on Twitter and many forums, and it's exhausting because as much as you can help change and help support behavioral change in one aspect, you turn around and you see an entire community of folks who are resilient and don't see that perspective. I think because the work is never done and because the work is fighting the systemic nature of oppression, that there truly couldn't be more difficult work out there. So that's what I mean by exhaustion. Even with all of that, I see Kim endure and again, to get personal, not only is she doing it on the behalf of the community, but she also does it on behalf of herself. This is her lived experience. So the work itself, I can only imagine, is exhausting, draining, and deeply personal.

## Why is this work necessary right now?

I think Kim's work is critical, especially now, because the workplace has changed and evolved in a way that not everyone fully comprehends. I think we are at the advent of an entire revolution in how businesses operate, and I think that what Kim introduces is a value-based way of thinking. Prioritizing values within a company and the values of the folx who work for you is the only path to deliver the supremacy-free, coercion-free, oppression-free future that our communities deserve. With the great resignation just happening and with so many folx having the opportunity to personally audit themselves during the pandemic, companies are reeling. They are, in effect, starting over as it relates to building their culture, their practices, and in some cases their entire business model. Their business model has been shaken: They have no idea what is happening. We see this happening in so many sectors, especially technology. It's impossible to calculate consumption habits, the rush to digital.

Everyone assumed that this digital revolution was expedited by five to 10 years because of COVID, and that's not playing out from a consumer perspective. There are just so many things that businesses and business leaders aren't able to forecast, so it's really topsy-turvy right now. The only way we are going to survive what's to come is to stop prioritizing the bottom line and start prioritizing our own folx who are the key and ticket to our bottom line and growth. If we do not stop, then there is no way the big companies are going to climb out of this, and small companies too. There is so much talk about what it means to live in a capitalist society on the heels of COVID, and we just aren't not getting it right. This is a tremendous opportunity for this work to get it right. I say from that perspective, it is critical because the sound and prudent economic model forward is to invest in your folx and let them show up as themselves. Figure out how to so they are delivering their best and that you are building happy, healthy companies so they will thrive inherently because of the folx and resources that are running them. So there is that aspect of it. The other reason it's so critical is that with the pressure that these companies face, the first things to go are these ancillary programs. When layoffs happen, they don't layoff those who they believe are critical to the supply chain or critical to product development. They layoff those who are doing the work that fosters these communities and this type of environment. So this work and any of the progress that has been made over the last few years could very easily fall to the wayside. The priority has to be solving workplace oppression, and so that is why I believe that this work is so critical right now. Frankly, there is not a lot of time. Kim's approach, which as we said is straightforward and direct, is really what needs to happen. We cannot sugarcoat what is happening anymore. We need to own it, we need to ask companies to own it, we need to ask companies to accept that they are fallible, Every organization and person has more work to do, including myself.

The sooner we can have these authentic conversations and are modeling the right type of conversations that should be happening at the leader-level, at the management-level, at every level of the organization, we can start to normalize that and make it part of the conversation and part of the business plan. We will all be better for it.

## Final thoughts

The only thing I want to do is express my gratitude. I am just grateful for the opportunity to know Kim and to work with Kim. I find that even in that gratitude, I have to be careful because I don't want to center my feelings, but I am grateful for the opportunity. Circling back to the conversation about the nature of how difficult the work is for Kim, I want to add that even with the amount of trauma that I believe Kim endures on the behalf of others by working through oppression, I believe that she does a wonderful job of finding hope, levity, and fun in her community. That is inspirational. I think that she also extends huge amounts of grace to those of us with much work left to do. When she extends grace or when she discusses herself as fallible, it helps folks connect with her as not only an educator and a role model but as a person. I think her ability to do that and reach deep within and live a joyful life is really admirable, and it's great to see.

# Ask Yourself

- How well do you know yourself?
- What would a regular "self-reflection" practice look like for you?
- Do you know your value outside of the systems, institutions, and policies that govern your life?
- How has work impacted your identity?
- Does the color of your skin have an impact on how you view yourself?
- Do you believe in the ability of folx to change?
- Is it possible to fully know yourself?
- Do you let friends/family get close to you?
- How do you set boundaries for yourself and others?
- Are you aware of your ability to leverage systems, institutions, and policies in ways that others are not?
- Do you understand the concept of "relative privilege?" In any given situation, do you recognize your ability to leverage systems, institutions, and policy changes?
- Do you know how to acknowledge when you've caused harm and apologize without centering yourself?
- What does a supremacy-, coercion-, discrimination-, and exploitation-free future look like to you?
- Are you willing to adopt a consistent, demonstrated, anti-racist practice?

# II. Know Thy Organization

"Be the change you want to see by shutting the
fuck up sometimes and getting to work."

Kim Crayton

# My Story

Entering tech in 2014 changed my life. As a consumer, I have always been curious about technology but this shift to a producer's perspective, where everything was new, often made me feel like a kid in a candy store...so many choices; so much to learn. But it wasn't until I started attending technology events that I realized something was explicitly different. For the first time, I heard folx talking about privilege, inclusion, and diversity and how their lack was now impacting the industry as a whole.

Due to these dynamics, they were fucking up, causing harm. They talked about how the lack of diversity, equity, and inclusion had created industry-wide crisis-management issues. How the collective ethos of "move fast, break things" had accelerated that harm. As with most systems, institutions, and policies, by the time folx started to recognize the problem, harm was being inflicted globally, at scale.

In tech, someone can code something, put it out on the internet, and instantly there can be problems. The lack of accessible technology is a great example. Folx regularly create products and services without giving much, if any, consideration to the accessibility needs of users. Technology solutions that completely leave out folx with low-vision or no-vision are not uncommon and do not seem like a big deal to some folx.

But it's exclusionary, and now folx who rely on such assistance are left out; they can't participate. My frustration with the lack of inclusion and the harmful impact that results is why I started #causeascene.

I began speaking at local tech meetings in 2016 because, as an educator who like many others, struggled with learning to code, I realized that vital adult-learning considerations were absent from how education was addressed. So much of the narrative within the industry in the effort to "fill the pipeline" appeared to have been adopted from a tech product/service pitch approach of championing "how easy it is," which I soon discovered was bullshit. Learning to code, like learning anything else, is a complex process requiring the learner to take in information. With time and practice, a solid knowledge and skill set is developed but what I and others were experiencing was not that. We experienced "curricula" that rarely followed any adult-learning theory, which resulted in folx internalizing our failures and deciding that "tech was not for me" instead of correctly questioning the quality of instruction. This attrition issue was most profoundly found among self-taught learners, those who came into the field without a traditional computer science background but with years of valuable experience and knowledge from other areas. So the most logical topic to speak about, which I knew would add value by addressing this issue, was mentoring.

With each talk, I became better known. As I shared more of my background and expertise on matters beyond mentoring, folx would be like, "Oh, I want you to talk about that," but there was little financial support for doing so. All around me, I saw white folx getting paid to speak, but folx not only expected me to speak for free, they often seemed offended when I asked to get paid for what had become my work. Folx wanted me to speak in different countries when I literally had no money in my account.

I can remember when I first started speaking, they would book me in a hotel and because I didn't have a credit card—all I had was a debit card—they would put a hold on my account. I was in a city I didn't know with barely any money to eat. I was flying around the world speaking and I didn't even have the funds to participate in some of the scheduled events or explore the city. It took these experiences for me to recognize and internalize that I was having a vastly different experience than many of the other speakers I met and that massive inequities were at play.

So when I started producing my own events, I understood the importance of removing as many barriers as possible. I understood that scholarship recipients shouldn't have to disclose that they didn't have money in their account, especially if my goal was to improve inclusion and diversity by including folx who traditionally weren't in the room. One, that is none of my business and two, their attendance was critical in achieving my intended goal. If you are providing a scholarship for the most vulnerable, you should be taking care of everything, and if one person wilds out at the mini-bar, big damn deal. That is the shit I saw that made me realize that these folx have no clue that their intentions, their efforts to help, were more than problematic, that they were actually causing harm.

Now they don't do that to me anymore, but I see it happening to others, especially during Black history month and Juneteenth. They want Black folks to talk, but they don't want to pay. My question for folx who think that doing anything for the common good should be done "out of the kindness of your heart and for no pay," is "Don't you expect to get paid when you go to work?" If you value this work, as you claim, why wouldn't you prioritize ensuring that those you are "hiring" to do this critical work are financially benfiting from their effort?

# My Truths

I know I can teach anybody how to build a business that is fundamentally rooted in not causing harm. I'm not going to say it's going to be absent of harm, but my focus is to minimize harm, and it's going to be profitable. I know my shit. I know when something is a training issue and when it's not. I know how to write curricula. I understand adult learning theory. I'm a researcher who learns best through lived experiences, experimentation, and the development of practical applications for testing theory. I found my opportunity to test my business development theory with Doc and Paul from Tito, whom I met as a speaker at their Admission conference, and who agreed to become the first sponsors of the #causeascene podcast in 2019. In exchange for being a financial sponsor, I offered to help them develop the policies, processes, and procedures that were missing from their organization. An engagement that was only supposed to last six weeks is still going strong in 2022. They, along with other entrepreneurs, were my guinea pigs for the content of my work and this book.

I started the International Tech Business Sustainability Scholarship (ITBSS) to test my ideas with people who don't speak English as their first language. I offered one underrepresented international organization leader 20 hours of advising services per quarter to help them build the framework for a successful business structure. This offer led me to work with a fantastic team in El Salvador at Unplug Studios. We all wanted to help as many struggling entrepreneurs as possible, so we decided that in exchange for my help, the Unplug Studio team would use our recorded sessions to make a reality-style show. This was because I wanted to find clever ways to show people how to build a business. And to be honest, developing and leveraging creative ways to teach business development is why I love this work.

I love bearing witness to the diversity of companies and ideas while taking folx through this process. Seeing others come up with concepts that I would never have considered fascinates me. It scratches an itch to where I am never bored. I was an entrepreneur at heart without the knowledge and skills of an entrepreneur, so I intimately understand the frustration that comes with being unable to move from idea to business success effectively.

Developing business ideas and several accompanying strategies comes easy to me. My head and notes app are filled wity fleshed out solutions to problems and opportunities, great and small. I can see something and develop a strategy. I remember having this idea to enhance the television football viewing experience, and I do not like football. I was like, "Wow, what if viewers could control what view they got to see?" You bought into a service and decided which camera to view that field goal from, which camera/s to view the replay, and which camera to view the halftime show. The fan got to create their own football viewing experience.

But like many other entrepreneurs, I didn't get to build that business or even test my idea because I couldn't access the basic information or resources that only a few can leverage. So I end up building low-barrier-to-entry service businesses. Businesses that don't require friends and family or VC investments that I can't access but that also don't scale well because, as an individual, there are only so many hours I can spend advising, speaking, writing, leading, advocating, etc. So yes, I can easily develop business ideas with little or no effort, but I don't have the resources or support to execute most of them, and I am not alone.

Some may ask, "Why do you spend so much time pointing out the inconsistencies resulting from systems, institutions, and policies designed to privilege the few at the expense of the many?" Because doing so challenges the narrative that enables those with the ability to leverage their unearned power and privilege by casting the excluded as inept, lazy, or any other derogatory description used to justify their "greatness" and our failings. As someone who studies whiteness at the intersection of business and understands that it is only allowed to be cast as a hero or a victim, never as the villain, I know that our silence is used as an agreement when we don't speak up or when we aren't in the room. White folx assume it's because we don't want to be there or aren't qualified to be there. No! We're not there because we don't have an entry.

What did Zora Neal Hurston say? "If you are silent about your pain, they will kill you and say you enjoyed it." I think about this a lot because that is what you hear. "Oh, we don't have any issues with our marginalized and vulnerable community members; there is no problem there." Whiteness "assumes" that, like itself, if these folx didn't feel safe or had concerns, they would say so, which leads white folx to assume there must not be any. I use "assume" here very loosely because, increasingly, due to our more connected society, white folx are becoming very aware that everyone is not having the same lived experiences. Once you know the reality of what it means to live as a Black or brown folx who is subjected to the violence of white supremacy and anti-Blackness, you can't unknow. We must all invest in addressing our internalized white supremacy and anti-Blackness. Due to our collective indoctrination, white folx must grapple with the fact that it would be reckless for most marginalized folx to trust you. You must realize that silence does not imply agreement or the absence of harm.

One of the folx I interviewed for my doctorate said he made an announcement in the company about who wanted a mentor, and all these folx got real loud, saying I don't want it. He said when he went back to his office, he started getting emails and direct messages from quieter folx saying yes, I would love mentoring. For context, I'm sharing this conversation as an example of how easy it is to assume silence equals agreement or complicence and the harm that such an assumption can cause.

At the end of the day, I am just a bad bitch. And I am ready to put it out there. That is why I can tell whiteness, particularly white dudes, to shut the fuck up. To say with my full chest that you are not my competition. You are the by-product of systems, institutions, and policies designed to ensure that you can access networks and resources that are denied to me. The vast majority of white folx are not winning by embracing "whiteness" because it doesn't allow them to develop the knowledge and skills to be their best. So mediocre and unremarkable are the result. The white supremacist narrative of "greatness, genius, and special" is quickly challenged when they're finally in the presence of folx who have been told our whole lives that we have to do 110% to get in the door. So no, whiteness is not my equal.

# Our Truths

We first need to understand that business decisions continue to reflect that organizational leaders are still operating as if we are in the Industrial Age where you gave someone a binder, pointed them to an assembly line, and told them to make widgets. We are in a knowledge economy. What we bring to the job, our lived experiences, is what organizational leaders need to innovate and compete. If we don't feel we are being respected and valued, our workplace can be on fire and we will not say a word; we will just grab our shit and leave. That's a power we've never had before. In the past, with top-down communication, leaders would dictate the rules and we would follow them without voicing our concerns. The problem is that companies refuse to accept that new reality because it would mean admitting that employees have more leverage than they want them to have. They want us to be good lab rats that do what they tell us to do, make our little salary, keep heads down and mouths shut. But we have more power now, and it's scaring the shit out of these organizational leaders. We need to push them out of their comfort zone so that we can start making real change.

Secondly, we now live in a very connected world. We never knew what was happening on the other side of the world unless we visited or someone from there told us. Now we can see it for ourselves, and what we thought were our unique experiences of being targets of harm, we've realized aren't so unusual. Thanks to social media, we are not as ignorant as we used to be. We need to develop strategies to capitalize on our ability to access new information, make connections, build community, and advocate for change within our organizations or build our own. We have never had this kind of leverage before. Today, it's entirely possible to build a business that doesn't have to depend on the "local" markets to be successful; of course, it might be preferred, but it is no longer required. Ford was a large company in the early 1900s, but that was an "American" car that only made it overseas in a limited capacity. We can start an online business and, on day one, make our target audience Japan. To be multinational, we no longer need to be a Fortune 500 company. Technology and access to information have aided in leveling the playing field for entrepreneurs and workers.

# Common Myths

A product or service is not a business. All too often, organizations fail, can't scale, or become toxic because their leaders don't understand that strategic and manageable growth requires policies, processes, and procedures that enable connectedness, innovation, and competitive advantage. Successful organizations are built on a foundation that helps their leaders transform information into knowledge to scale, evolve, and recover. The ability of organizational leaders to successfully create and manage operations relies heavily on how well they develop these necessary policies, processes, and procedures. When leaders take the time to understand and operationalize their organization's functions, they avoid common barriers to success while recovering more quickly from unexpected events. Building a thriving organization with fewer unintended consequences requires more than a great product or service. It requires leaders to be able to give all stakeholders the experiences they want and the ability to manage the process.

## Stakeholders:

1. Those who work for you;

2.  Those who partner with you;
3.  Those who buy from you;
4.  Those who are impacted by you; and
5.  Those who invest in you.

Going from product/service to a business model focus takes time, intention, and strategic effort. All are necessary to innovate, differentiate, and compete in the Information Age. Also, building stakeholder-focused rather than shareholder-focused organizations is a proactive approach to addressing inclusion, diversity, equity, safe spaces, and developing a harm-reduction perspective. When leaders create organizations around well-defined and tested core values that consider the needs of all stakeholders and have processes in place to monitor progress, they are less likely to discover, at some point in the future, that they've been nurturing an exclusionary environment with unintended consequences.

Establishing the necessary policies, processes, and procedures also enables business leaders to shift from working in their businesses to working on their businesses. What's the difference? Working in your business means you've transferred responsibility for managing your position and obligations from within an organization to yourself; you've created a job for yourself. How do you know if you've created a job for yourself? Can the work get done without you? If you can not hand your roles and responsibilities over to someone else, you have created a job for yourself. There is nothing wrong with that, but folx need to understand the difference because they impact decision-making. A good example here is a law firm. Out of necessity, a firm with one or two attorneys who handle every aspect of the client relationship operates differently than one with staff hired to handle specific functions within that relationship. So, although you may comply with all local, state, and federal government rules related to operating as a business, i.e., licenses, taxes, contracts, etc., your ability to access funding, scale, and compete is fundamentally limited depending on your capacity. So deciding whether you desire to scale beyond your capacity is essential to determining which policies, processes, and procedures will aid your success.

Building a business in a knowledge economy that relies on organizational leaders' ability to leverage the lived experiences of stakeholders requires that attention be paid to operationalizing its core values into policies, processes, and procedures. It requires that organizational leaders recognize, acknowledge, and create strategies to mitigate the harm that's inflicted on the most vulnerable due to systems, institutions, and policies that are designed to privilege the few at the expense of the many. It requires adopting a community of learning and practice that prioritizes harm reduction. It requires an understanding that without welcoming and psychological safety, they are actively contributing to circumstances that lead to risk, and increasingly, crisis-management issues.

# What You Need To Know

## LEARNING ORGANIZATION

*"The cause of many problems lay in the very well-intentioned policies designed to alleviate them."*

*The Fifth Element*

*Peter Senge*

So often, when advising clients on how to create the policies, processes, and procedures they need to meet their business goals, it doesn't take long to realize that our efforts will be hampered if barriers created by organizational leaders who are only focused on scaling a product or service aren't addressed.

Change is happening around us, yet most business decision-making processes are stuck in the Industrial Age. Wake up! We are in the Information Age, where welcoming and psychological safety are essential components of effective business development strategies. To succeed, we must take steps to shed the outdated thinking and organizational behaviors that only serve to maintain the status quo. Success in today's knowledge economy requires that all internal stakeholders understand how decisions impact business leaders' ability to innovate, differentiate, gain competitive advantage, and profit along with their role in meeting established benchmarks is key.

134

Effectively doing business in the Information Age requires a diversity of perspectives in order to create products and services that meet the needs of global customers and clients, while minimizing harm. To remain competitive, it is no longer wise to say, "We tried and it's not working." It's the business leaders who are committed to understanding why their efforts fail and learning from those failures who will be best positioned to leverage the knowledge gained to dominate in leading inclusive organizations. As a result, building business operations from a learning organization viewpoint that enables organizational leaders to harness internal and external knowledge should be a top focus.

## The Disciplines of the Learning Organization:

- Systems Thinking
- Personal Mastery
- Mental Models
- Building Shared Vision
- Team Learning

## The Laws of the Fifth Discipline — Problem Truths (*The Fifth Element*, Peter Senge)

1. Today's problems come from yesterday's "solutions."
2. The harder you push, the harder the system pushes back.
3. Behavior grows better before it grows worse.
4. The easy way out usually leads back in.
5. The cure can be worse than the disease.
6. Faster is slower.
7. Cause and effect are not closely related in time and space.

8.  Small changes can produce big results but the areas of highest leverage are often the least obvious.
9.  You can have your cake and eat it too but not at once.
10. Dividing an elephant in half does not produce two small elephants.
11. There is no blame.

# Systems Thinking

> *"Business and other human endeavors are also systems. They, too, are bound by invisible fabrics of interrelated actions, which often take years to fully play out their effects on each other. Since we are part of that lacework ourselves, it's doubly hard to see the whole pattern of change. Instead, we tend to focus on snapshots of isolated parts of the system, and wonder why our deepest problems never seem to get solved."*

*The Fifth Element*
*Peter Senge*

Far too often, the challenges we face within our organizations result from "siloed thinking." Individuals, teams, and divisions operate with little to no understanding or consideration of how they impact the whole. This limited perspective approach and the inability to forecast one's potential impact on all organizational stakeholders means that short- and long-term planning efforts lack the insight needed to spot unexpected opportunities and looming risks.

# Personal Mastery

*"Personal mastery is the discipline of continually clarifying and deepening your personal vision, of focusing our energies, of developing patience, and of seeing reality objectively. As such, it is an essential cornerstone of the learning organization, the learning organization's spiritual foundation. An organization's commitment to and capacity for learning can be no greater than that of its members."*

*The Fifth Element*

*Peter Senge*

As a multipotentialite, it is my nature to be curious, to question, and seek answers to those questions. I am an "extreme generalist," which means that I can go very deep and then pull back on a variety of subject matter, enabling me to connect the dots across many domains [systems thinking]. It is a desire for personal mastery that guides me. Personal mastery enables organizational leaders to leverage the lived experiences of their stakeholders to innovate, differentiate, and compete. The ability to benefit organizationally from personal mastery is also why welcoming and psychological safety are essential components for establishing a culture that fosters the conditions for personal mastery. It is important to realize that a learning organization, which is internally focused on the capacity to capture and share the knowledge gained from data derived from the lived experiences of relevant stakeholders, differs from organizational learning, which is externally focused on training, workshops, team-building activities, etc. So instead of the "pour in" processes that dominated in the Industrial Age, a learning organization requires an appropriate relationship-building strategy because if stakeholders don't feel safe enough to share, the effort and resources to encourage personal mastery are wasted.

# Mental Models

> *"'Mental models' are deeply ingrained*
> *assumptions, generalizations, or even pictures*
> *or images that influence how we understand*
> *the world and how we take action."*
>
> The Fifth Element
> *Peter Senge*

The problem with mental models is that they influence how we interact with the outside world, but they are rarely critically scrutinized. Codifying the unquestioned mental models of those in positions of power and influence that tell others how to act without their knowledge or consent and then holding them accountable for it or evaluating them on it is a big reason why many people don't feel welcomed and psychologically safe at work. Because of this, requests for "empathy," "giving the benefit of the doubt," and "assuming good intent," especially during a risk or crisis event, increase the possibility of harm. On the surface, these requests for "understanding" might seem to be the way to reconciliation and improved relations, but what they enable problematic and harmful behavior resulting in professional violence, and frequently give permission to the already privileged and powerful to avoid taking responsibility for their actions by never having to evaluate their mental models and the impact they have on others.

# Building Shared Vision

*"One is hard pressed to think of any organization that has sustained some measure of greatness in the absence of goals, values, and missions that become deeply shared throughout the organization. The practice of shared vision involves the skills of unearthing shared 'pictures of the future' that foster genuine commitment and enrollment rather than compliance. In mastering this discipline, leaders learn the counterproductiveness of trying to dictate a vision, no matter how heartfelt."*

The Fifth Element

*Peter Senge*

Establishing a culture of shared values has always been an essential technique for ensuring that cohesion results from the combined efforts of individuals. It's one thing to have stated values posted on marketing materials and another to reflect them in the finished product or service and how one engages with relevant stakeholders. The ability of organizational leaders to provide evidence of the operationalization of shared values enables them to chart a clearer, less ambiguous path toward leveraging organizational knowledge for innovation, differentiation, and gaining a competitive advantage.

Due to this understanding, I knew that shifting my work and the community away from #causeascene, which was about calling out white supremacy and anti-Blackness, to Profit Without Oppression required the development of a new set of shared [core] values. Where #causeascene was about "what was/is," Profit Without Oppression is about the possibility of "what could be." I knew that our continued focus on "what was/is" would never lead to our desired end...a future that is supremacy-, coercion-, discrimination-, and exploitation-free. The adoption of a shared vision of the future ignited my energy and this work. The ability that we now have to work collaboratively across affinity groups and domain interests, as long as our work is rooted in building a supremacy-, coercion-, discrimination-, and exploitation-free future, has become the gateway to welcoming and psychological safety that's been missing.

# Team Learning

"We know that teams can learn; in sports, in the performing arts, in science, and even occasionally, in business, there are striking examples where the intelligence of the team exceeds the intelligence of the individuals in the team, and where teams develop extraordinary capacities for coordinated action. When teams are truly learning, not only are they producing extraordinary results but the individual members are growing more rapidly than could have occurred otherwise."

*The Fifth Element*

*Peter Senge*

Team learning is essential to building a successful business in a knowledge economy, but I often see it as the most likely place for things to go wrong and cause the most damage to stakeholders. This is because real learning requires a level of welcoming and psychological safety that most organizations don't have. Benefiting from team learning requires folx to be encouraged and challenged in ways that facilitate growth without unnecessary trauma. Effective and efficient team learning is a product of developing, operationalizing, and measuring core values in ways that create a shared ethos of respect at every organizational level, where the most powerful and privileged understand that their destiny is tied to the success of the marginalized and most vulnerable because it is through the knowledge gained from their lived experiences that the creation of products and services that provide value to all stakeholders with minimal harm lies. Unfortunately, most "team learning" efforts evolve out of a need to keep the most powerful comfortable and, in doing so, eliminate any chance of abandoning the status quo.

Team learning that prioritizes a supremacy-, coercion-, discrimination-, and exploitation-free experience doesn't happen just because the stated culture is "family." In fact, "family" is often the first place we learn to accept mental, physical, emotional, and spiritual abuse as love. It's this false narrative of "family" that folx who benefit exclusively from the "assumption of positive intent" rely on to escape accountability; it's manipulative and ensures the failure of any efforts toward welcoming and psychological safety. This is at the heart of the continual failure of diversity, equity, and inclusion efforts.

Another barrier to team learning is siloed rather than systems thinking. Too often in these streets, you have one group of individuals, usually white dudes, whose effort and contributions are prized over everyone else's. These individuals are allowed to keep their heads down and only think about their work. They don't have to consider how their work affects others in or outside their domain. These individuals are lauded as essential, "technical." They are more valued and are seldom held to the same standard of behavior as others...so much so that their often documented harmful behavior is justified, accommodated, and prioritized over the needs of others. Team learning rooted in a supremacy-, coercion-, discrimination-, and exploitation-free organizational ethos requires that all stakeholders take personal responsibility for monitoring the environment and challenging potential barriers to the team learning dynamic while managing their feelings.

# 6-Step Business Development Strategy

Moving from a product and service model to a business operations model focus requires a series of intentional and strategic steps. The first step is to imagine. I have my clients imagine the ideal stakeholder experience and write it down in detail. This assignment is not an outlining session but focused on how you want stakeholders to feel. This is a time to tap into their emotions and forget about their product or service. I usually don't have clients talk about their product or service until after several sessions. I do this because entrepreneurs can become married to a product or service, which gets them in trouble and limits business leaders' vision of what's possible. They hold onto it regardless of how it impacts stakeholders.

Step two is to define. You want to have a company ethos that drives your decisions and work. These sessions are where you define your core values and what that experience looks like for stakeholders. You then have to define the indicators you need that let you know that stakeholders are having the experience you imagined in step one. What policies, processes, and procedures need to be developed to help ensure that stakeholders have the intended experiences? For me, some of those indicators that let me know that my stakeholders are having the intended experiences with understanding and adopting a supremacy-, coercion-, discrimination-, and exploitation-free ethos include meeting or exceeding my monthly income goals because I've secured new advising clients. I know I am getting attention and have significant growth in brand awareness because I am getting more followers on social media, podcast invites, media interviews, and more folx are inviting me to their conferences and are attending my events.

Step three is to apply measurements to indicators. For myself, the indicator that I am getting clients is X dollars per month by a specific date. The indicator that I am getting more attention is measured by a goal of being a guest on X number of podcasts by a specific date. I must reach this benchmark to claim success. Step three is where you develop effective metrics for measuring core values. You are creating the tools to convert the intangible to the tangible.

Step four is to test. Test the indicators with your stakeholders by collecting both quantitative and qualitative data and feedback. Both are necessary to obtain a more "rounded" and complete picture.

Step five is to evaluate measurements to determine if benchmarks were met. If they were met, why? If they weren't met, why? Use this knowledge that you have gained from the evaluation of the test to refine the process.

Step six is to standardize that. Create formal processes based on knowledge gained from evaluation. Document and share both explicit and tacit knowledge. Documentation is one of the first ways to be more inclusive in your communities. You must write documentation, particularly if your stakeholders use it to answer their questions. Your documentation is not a "one-and-done" thing. It should be treated as living, ever-changing. You also need to develop efficient and effective strategies and processes for sharing tacit knowledge. Tacit knowledge is the knowledge someone gains from doing a task numerous times and coming up with a system to complete it. Tacit knowledge is gained through lived experience and that knowledge must be shared throughout the organization. In an information economy, it is tacit knowledge, not books or binders, that will enable organizational leaders to differentiate and be competitive.

There are some important considerations for these steps. Core values should inform all organizational decisions. It would help if you were mindful that this is an ongoing and not concrete process. The conclusions resulting from this process should not be seen as immutable or rigid. Finally, organizational leaders should plan to review at least twice a year whether stakeholder factors have changed. This will enable them to anticipate shifting needs and to proactively plan accordingly.

# You Can't Manage What You Can't Measure

You cannot manage what you cannot measure. Developing efficient and effective processes for measuring outcomes is essential for leveraging data for innovation, gaining a competitive advantage, and mitigating risk.

## One of the appeals of owning a franchise is the established policies, processes, and procedures.

The ability of organizational leaders to successfully create and manage operations relies heavily on how well they develop the necessary processes. When leaders take the time to understand and operationalize their organization's functions, they avoid common barriers to success while recovering more quickly from unexpected events. Unexpected things will happen. When you are building a business, you are testing stuff out. You may believe that you've gotten all your ducks in a row only to wake up to discover that your site has been hacked, an employee has been charged with insider trading, or filmed on their off-work time behaving in a manner that puts the entire organization at risk. Things will happen and having policies, processes, and procedures in place before they do allows you to prepare at least for some of those predictable unknowns. Yet far too many business leaders I've worked with have no policies, processes, or procedures. These leaders spend a lot of resources reinventing the wheel with each new hire or partner acquisition and definitely have no idea what to do when an unexpected chaotic event happens. Building a thriving organization with fewer unintended consequences requires more than a great product or service. It requires leaders to be able to give all stakeholders the experiences they want and the ability to manage the process.

## Our organizational stakeholders are [listed in order of priority]:

The chief concern of most organizational leaders who follow a traditional business model is maximizing shareholder/ownership value. In parts of the world that have adopted similar economic models, a company's board of directors or its CEO must prioritize maximizing shareholder value over all other considerations. Although violating this long-held tenet is not illegal, the idea in practice is treated as if it were. If business leaders make decisions or take action that could be seen to impede or isn't in the interest of realizing a maximization in that value or that would not bring the shareholders as much money as possible, shareholders could have legal remedies to hold them accountable. The company's shareholders own that company, and the CEO and board of directors are treated as stewards and are expected to do whatever they can, within the bounds of the law, to make sure that shareholders are not only not losing money but are maximizing their profits. This is why business leaders invest so many resources into lobbying Congress, the law-making body of government, to "assist" in writing and passing laws that benefit their business interests.

Shifting to stakeholder focus means prioritizing maximizing shareholder value, although important, isn't organizational leaders' only concern. They must also consider the organizational impact beyond those with an ownership stake.

Prioritizing stakeholder value is essential for adopting a business operations model which aids us in scaling the Profit Without Oppression framework. These stakeholders are:

1.  Those who work for you;
2.  Those who partner with you;
3.  Those who buy from you;
4.  Those who are impacted by you; and
5.  Those who invest in you.

I've arranged the list of stakeholders in this way for a reason. The employees who work for you are your most important asset. They determine how successful business leaders will be at meeting their organizational goals. Much consideration must be given to improving the experiences of those internal stakeholders because they are the folx with the knowledge and skills that enable organizational leaders to innovate, differentiate, and gain a competitive advantage. Along with internal concerns, who to partner with will impact the products and services you intend to bring to the marketplace. When adopting a stakeholder perspective, more must be considered besides the cost of goods sold. In an increasingly connected world, your partner's missteps can quickly become an unexpected risk or crisis-management issue.

Next is who buys from you. We all know that everybody will not become a customer; therefore, it's crucial to identify and test your assumptions about customer acquisition and retention. This includes assessing whether your customer base aligns with your stated core values. Operating from a traditional business model, it is unheard of to shift away or drop a problematic customer demographic. But the ability to do so, rooted in a desire to build a supremacy-, coercion-, discrimination-, and exploitation-free future helps organizational leaders keep the promises they may have made to other stakeholders. There are some clients you will not want, but you can't know that or articulate that well if you have not made these determinations or thought about these things.

Organizational leaders who take an interest in understanding their business's impact on known and unknown stakeholders are taking critical steps to ensure that what they're building is profitable and rooted in harm reduction. Organizational leaders often find themselves in situations where they're "surprised" to learn of their product's or service's harmful impact via social media or the news. Without some understanding of the potential for harm, they find themselves in unfamiliar and unpopular situations that have spun out of their ability to manage. The final consideration is for those who invest in you. If you've effectively developed your understanding of and relationships with the first four stakeholder groups, their investments will be protected because you'll have positioned your business for profitability while minimizing potential negative impacts.

## Prioritize Stakeholder Value, Community, Minimizing Harm, & The Most Vulnerable

When leaders build organizations around well-defined and tested core values that consider the needs of all stakeholders and have processes in place to monitor progress, they are less likely to discover, at some point in the future, that they've been nurturing an exclusionary and harmful environment. Building stakeholder value rather than shareholder-only focused organizations is a proactive approach to addressing inclusion, equity, diversity, welcoming and psychological safety, innovation, and profitability. Our efforts in these areas must be intentional and strategic to help minimize the potential that our actions might harm underrepresented and marginalized individuals. The continued lack of diversity is one of my main issues with the developer Q&A platform Stack Overflow. Their annual research survey data from 2016-2022 indicates that most respondents were white males/men between 18 to 34. The number one issue I have with the Stack Overflow annual survey is that business leaders use this data to draw conclusions and make decisions on the larger, more diverse, global community without evaluating deeply why the lack of diversity exists among survey respondents. The only reliable and ethical conclusions drawn from this data would be limited to white males/men aged 18-34, which means that once again, the needs of and the opportunities to mitigate harm for the underrepresented and marginalized remain unknown or ignored.

## Building Organizations: Floor [Define core values], Walls [Operationalize core values], Roof [Measure core values]

Building a supremacy-, coercion-, discrimination-, and exploitation-free future requires intentional and strategic effort. It requires folx in every role to understand the need to prioritize the most vulnerable and minimize harm. It requires business leaders to focus the development of their organizations in ways that reflect an understanding of the need to define, operationalize, and measure core values. You can approach the development of this process as one would follow a blueprint to build a house. Blueprints are a universal way to document common elements shared among houses: floors, walls, and a roof, and those additional elements that distinguish one house from another: floor, wall, and roof type. The ability to adhere to the blueprint helps ensure that all stakeholders have a common understanding of how the elements of any given house are constructed. The blueprint becomes the de facto tool for communicating effectively and efficiently among those tasked with the building's completion and ongoing maintenance. Core values, like blueprints, provide organizational leaders with a clear way forward.

## These commonalities are not new. The difference is developing core values from a supremacy-, coercion-, discrimination-, and exploitation-free framework.

The process of developing organizational core values is not new. This process is so common that it is often undertaken as a PR/marketing exercise without much thought given to how core values can and should be used to make decisions related to every part of business operations. Once developed, they should be treated as organizational guideposts. Given time, all stakeholders soon realize the benefit that having well-defined and widely communicated core values brings to making all manner of decisions, from the simple to the complex. From choosing appropriate supply chain partners to how to treat those who work for you, if the economic climate necessitates layoffs. And organizational leaders that employ a supremacy-, coercion-, discrimination-, and exploitation-free lens to construct their core values find they have laid the framework for work and relationships that can navigate business competition with fewer unintended consequences.

## 3 PILLARS FOR COMPETITIVE ADVANTAGE IN ORGANIZATIONS IN A KNOWLEDGE ECONOMY

Leadership (Develop = Lead)
Management (Direct = Manage)

Stakeholders (Deliver = Execute)

1. Core Values (Leadership)
   1. Move from Intention to Strategy
      1. Imagine
      2. Define
      3. Apply
      4. Test
      5. Evaluate
      6. Standardization
   2. Communicate Values
   3. Allocate Resources
2. Organizational Structure (Management)
   1. Shift in Perspective From Industrial Age to Information Age
      1. We are no longer making widgets, but we still hire and manage as if we are. We need to hire for lived experience and manage the ability to turn information into organizational knowledge.
      2. We need to ensure that everyone in the organization knows their role/s and responsibilities and how their work impacts overall organizational success.
      3. The effective communication of policies, procedures, protocols, and processes that are tied to indicators and measurements are essential in enabling employees to align their efforts in meeting organizational goals.
   2. Screen For the Knowledge and Skills Needed for Innovation, Differentiation, and Competitive Advantage (Recruiting, Onboarding, Retaining, and Offboarding)
   3. Management Training Components:
      1. Guiding Principles

2. Rules of Engagement
3. Manage Your Feelings
3. Organizational Community (Stakeholders)
    1. Work For You (Internal)
        1. Clearly defined and articulated expectations
        2. Training
        3. Mentoring
    2. Partners With You (External)
    3. Buy From You (External)
    4. Impacted by You (External)
    5. Invest in You (External)

# Caveat: Corporate Blackface

*The idea that corporations publicly declare support of the Black Lives Matter movement, often with vague language and no publicly shared strategic plan, without actually committing to or implementing real, systemic change within their company to support Black employees, clients, customers, and community*

## EXAMPLES

*When a company:*

- *releases statements, claiming to support Black lives, but fails to fix the toxicity and discrimination against Black folx within their own company culture*
- *openly showcases illustrations and or stock photography of Black folx in its marketing materials, but doesn't actually include them in any of its teams and/or user research, leadership, or decision-making roles*
- *has an all-white leadership team and tweets about its support of Black Lives Matter without addressing its complicity in maintaining systems, institutions, and policies of white supremacy and anti-Blackness*

- *does little to impact policy that disproportionately and negatively influences their Black employees, clients, and/or customers*
- *claims to care about diversity and representation but then retaliates against/terminates a Black employee for identifying and speaking out on anti-Blackness they experience in the workplace*
- *no longer actively tries to increase diversity and inclusion in their company after Black Lives Matter is no longer trending on social media*

*While the list above is finite, there are many more ways that corporations show again and again that they only really care about their image rather than Black lives.*

# Commentary

"Know Thy Organization" is a six-step process toward operationalizing your organization's core values, the first step of which is to Imagine. I take clients through a process where I want them just to dream big with no limitations. This step is usually the first time folx consciously realize the number of limitations they put on themselves, their ideas, and their ability to dream, particularly folx from marginalized and vulnerable communities. Even giving the specific and explicit instructions that they have no barriers to resources, that the sky is the limit, they still dream so small.

It is this first step, I provide as little guidance as needed for them to understand the assignment. I'm able to start addressing some of the self-imposed challenges many entrepreneurs face due to systems, institutions, and policies that have been designed to privilege and elevate the ideas of the few, while sowing the seeds of self-doubt for the many. My instructions here are clear and simple: Write down in as much detail as possible what their ideal client-customer interaction looks like and oh my God, when they come back, what they share is so small. I love this part because it lets them see how small they've been making their dreams. Even after being told that there are no limitations, look how small you made your idea; your "success."

Once I've gotten them past their internalized limits, we'll define the indicators they'll need for a customer to have the best experience possible. "What does that look like?" We develop core values from there. Then we work on converting indicators into measurements. So, how would it look? They may state, "We must achieve this benchmark to claim success," and this is how they will align and measure their core values. "You can't manage what you can't measure," period. They must test those indicators before evaluating the measurement to see if their benchmarks were met. If so, why? if not, why not? Then, using this knowledge, refine and test the results. Standardization is the final step. It develops formal processes based on evaluation stage knowledge, documents explicit knowledge, shares tacit knowledge, and iterates on that process.

# Case Study: Twila

## When did you first meet Kim?

I met Kim a few years ago at the inaugural Blacks In Tech conference. I was moderating a panel and at the last minute, we had a person drop out. The replacement that they brought in was Kim. I literally met her about, I don't know, half-an-hour before we went on stage if that because it might even have been a shorter time frame. She was a part of a four-person panel. So it was Kim, a vice president from YouTube, an engineering executive from Buzzfeed, and the late rapper Nipsey Hussle. We were talking about the present state of the technology industry and Black people's representation in it. Once we got on stage and started talking and I started asking questions, Kim immediately became like a singular voice in that room. She was just a person whose ideas were so well defined and who had such a strong POV that everyone in the room just kept wanting to ask questions, follow back up to what she was talking about, and wanting her to go into more detail. I think my favorite moment happened when I posed a question to the entire panel. I directed it to Kim first and she answered the question thoroughly and eloquently with such a call to action that afterward, I asked Nipsey Hussle if he would like to respond as well. He jokingly said, *"I don't want to have to go after her."* The entire audience just laughed. Kim had this very just specific energy and drive. She wanted more for us. She was talking to that room in a way that explained that there is a path forward and here's what it looks like. It was very inspiring.

## What was the most impactful thing Kim shared on the panel?

I don't think it was one specific thing that she said. I think the most impactful thing she did was show a room full of young professionals, particularly Black professionals working in and attempting to work in the tech industry that they belonged there. This wasn't a matter of *"Oh, you have to fight to earn your place,"* or *"You have to work hard to get recognition."* Kim immediately made it clear that everyone in the room was already talented enough to do the work, that they are being acted upon by institutional and structural and external forces that make it difficult for Black people to reach and sustain and express the level of talent that we actually possess. I think for a lot of people, that was a revolutionary thought that it wasn't just *"Oh, you have to work twice as hard"* or *"You have to earn extra to hold validity."* She was telling everyone in that room, *"You have validity right now. The reason that your validity isn't expressed that way, the reason why you haven't gotten to the levels that we all deserve to be at, is because there are institutional structural biases and prejudices and racism that is being acted upon you every day."* But she didn't just say, *"Oh, you know, it's too bad. You know, life is hard for us."* What she was making sure to point out is that you have a place and you need to take action to make sure you're able to practice in that place. Every time she spoke, it was a rallying cry to that room, that each person deserved more, that

163

they have everything in them they need to do it, and that they have to understand how the systems and structures work in order to be able to execute it. I think for a lot of people, myself included, that was the first time we had really heard that in a way that wasn't expressed from sort of a baby boomer point of view. Like *"It's always gonna be hard. You can't win everything."* Or even a Generation X perspective, which is *"It's difficult, so we're just gonna find an alternate way to do it."* Kim was talking about setting the blocks in motion to change everything, not just how to make do with the systems we're already in.

## What is the necessity for a voice like Kim's in today's climate?

Kim's voice is necessary because we don't have enough people speaking on behalf of the community who are showing us how to get further. We get a lot of "work hard" advice. We get a lot of "these are the steps to success." Kim has pointed out to me that a lot of the systems that we invest in that we think are systems that can be used to better ourselves are based on the paradigms set by white people. So, we're not really forging our own path. What we're doing is forging a path that is set by white people that is meant to emulate white people and which we cannot succeed in because inherently they are threatened by the notion of us having success. So you go and you turn yourself inside out. You attempt to hit those markers that they set in the way they set them at their comfort level, and you still don't succeed. Kim pushes all of that aside. She uses her voice to tell you, *"You already have these things in your possession, you already have this talent and the skill."* She often talks about understanding, and I think this is my favorite quote that she says: *"Intention without strategy is chaos."* So when you understand that you have an intention, whatever that intention is, she does such a strong job of talking about the strategy that you need to make that

164

intention a reality in your every day. That is why a voice like hers is important. As Black people, as women, as marginalized people, we don't hear enough about taking the intention that we have, what we actually want for ourselves, and being able to put a strategy around them to be able to achieve those things. Whether those are ambitious goals or whether those are just you wanting to be able to work in your profession with a level of respect and engagement every day. She really understands how to make you see and think about that through a very clear lens, as opposed to trying to think under the weight of how white people have told you that you have to approach things.

## Why is it appropriate to be unapologetic when speaking about this particular topic?

I think it's important that Kim approaches her work in a way that is absolutely unapologetic because one of the things we need the most is to hear voices of people who don't apologize for just existing in the skin that they're in. Kim completely wipes that off the table. As women, as Black people, as people of color, as marginalized people, we are told continuously that there is something fundamentally off about us because of the group we came from. We know inherently that this is prejudices, racism, intolerance, and ignorance at play. But we have absorbed it. It has now become a part of our everyday DNA. We actually think these things about ourselves. A voice like Kim's cuts through all of that. She cuts through it so distinctly because she is unapologetic about herself and the space she holds in the world. And she's unapologetic about the space *we* deserve to hold in the world. If you don't have someone who can talk that way and speak truth to power that way, what happens is you get just that same sort of regurgitation of what white people say we should have in the way that white people feel comfortable letting us have it. That means you don't actually push for change, you don't actually push for progress. What you do is say *"Well, this takes time"* or *"Well, you have to use diplomacy."* Others say *"Well, there needs to be a certain amount of civility"* or *"There needs to be a certain amount of politeness that goes into any change of any process."* Kim makes a point to say all of those things have to be held with a very specific understanding that we deserve respect first. We hold space, and that's enough. Everything you build on that is based on that fundamental respect. It's not *"When you make me feel comfortable, I will respect you."*

## What do you believe the audience walked away from at the end of the Blacks In Tech conference and their interactions with Kim? What was the resounding message?

I think the resounding message is don't wait. Do not wait for white people. Do not. Do not wait for large-scale structures and institutions to validate you. You're already valid. You need to go out and build the thing you're going to build. You need to go out and invest in yourself in the way that you deserve to invest. You cannot wait for these other entities around you to give you permission to be yourself or to work successfully or to build and grow in your career. They're not going to give it to you. They're not. They're always going to move the goalpost. Don't wait for them. Hearing her tell a roomful of people that they have an actual source of power within themselves to make changes on behalf of themselves was transformational. Not just for everybody in the audience, but for me as an entrepreneur who came in to host as a favor to a friend. To sit there and feel like I got a whole word. And not just a word or a sermon, but something with action attached to it. I left that day thinking I need to know more and specifically to know this person. She needs to be a part of my life on a regular basis. And she is because I made

PROFIT WITHOUT OPPRESSION

sure to follow exactly what she said and engage with her in a way that helped create a long-term friendship.

## What do you say to Kim when you recognize that this work is not easy? What do you say to her to encourage her to continue?

Honestly, I think one of the reasons why I appreciate her friendship so much is because we are able to see in each other and in our group of friends when the other is having a struggle or mood or are caught and don't really know where to take their thinking next. The one thing I always try to remind her is she already knows everything she wants to do. Her vision is far and vast and wide and defined. She absolutely understands and is thinking 10 steps ahead of the rest of us. I think sometimes the hardest thing for her is wanting to be able to just execute everything now. And sometimes I think the hardest thing for her is understanding that it's okay for her as an individual to take the time she needs to rest, renew, and adjust to the ways that her vision is growing and changing. I'm always telling her, *"You know your own voice the most. You know yourself the best. You don't have to let anybody else, you know, push that or move that or try to make you feel like it's not the thing at the core that you know it to be."* Because sometimes she has ideas that are so big that I think even she has to step back and go, *"This is a very big idea. I think I'm supposed to be the one to do it. I don't always know how."* Giving yourself the space to say that creates space to just sit with it, let it come to you in its biggest form, and then act on it. That can sometimes be the scariest thing. I don't think Kim ever has to really worry and I don't actually think she spends time worrying about if something isn't going to work or if it's not going to succeed. I think the thing that she most concerns herself with is that she has to build the thing that can do the most good. As you can imagine, that's a lot of weight to put on one person's shoulders. But she is the type of person who wouldn't want that weight anywhere else. I feel like one of the things I'm called to do as her friend is to recognize when that weight is very heavy. I need to be there with a joke on a text or a long conversation when we haven't caught up or just remind her of a conversation we had before when she's struggling with a thought. I can point out because I've seen it. This is where that thought went before. You're right there. You're really close to it. It's to be of support to her as she does that. And I will tell you as much as I give, I get back equally because Kim is the kind of person who shows up immediately for you the same way that you show up for her. We both understand that this work is not easy. And I think the gift is knowing that the choice to do something that is hard that you are called to do is often filled with people who understand that as well and who can support you through that.

## Is there anything else you would like to say that has not been included?

I think one of the most important things to point out here is my relationship with Kim. While it started at the Blacks In Tech conference, the real growth and depth of our relationship occurred over general conversation where we were catching up with each other. I said very sort of offhandedly, *"I think I'm going to close my business."* I was struggling with it. I didn't have a lot of support or direction, and I was going through some stuff. Kim could have easily just turned that into a side comment from a friend where you just take the normal approach of *"I don't want to get into your mess."* She could have just said, *"I'm sorry to hear that. Is there anything I could do? Let me know if there's anything I could do."* Instead, what she did is the thing that she does so well. She stopped and she asked *"What is going on?"* She gave me space to just put it all out there and to just say, *"This is what's happening right now."* As a person who runs a business by herself, I didn't have a lot of outlets to just say, *"This is what's going wrong. I don't know what to do."* At the end of it, she said without hesitation, *"I'm going to start working with you."* And I said, "Ma'am, no, that's...You don't have to do that. And I certainly have no money to pay you." And she said, *"I didn't ask for your money. I said I'm going to help you with your business. I can see what's going on here. I can see where you need help. I'm going to help you."* Over the next four to five months, she met with me every week. She set a course of action to help me not just untangle the difficult thoughts I was having with the business but do something fundamental. She helped me take the thing I knew how to do, which is make audio, create structures so that I could replicate the process of making audio. I was very good at something, but not good at building a structure where that thing could be replicated. This is a very common thing in business, but a lot of us don't understand that, especially small-business owners and creative entrepreneurs like myself. Often Black small-business owners don't ever know that because we're not given access to systems and structures where we would learn about it. We're learning on our own. We're bootstrapping our own businesses. We're building as we go, and we don't always have that background. Because of her work with me, I was able to not only keep my business open but to grow it. Because of her work with me, I was not only able to grow my business but create a long-term vision for the business. And I will honestly say whether she wants to accept that or not, had it not been for the help she gave me, I would not have survived the pandemic. My business would have closed. But I had developed a structure and a system to work within, understood how to take care of the business, and how to continue to grow it even as business was stagnant and clients dried up. Even the mental thought process to not panic when those things started to happen came from working with her. She helped me understand that I needed to be able to look at the entire business and not be so far inside of it that I felt trapped by it. That was a gift that she gave me. It's a gift that continues to pay dividends. She'll never fully understand how much that meant to me. And I don't think she'll ever really fully understand how grateful I am that not only does she have this knowledge and understanding, but that she so easily and willingly shared it with me at a moment's notice. It's a gift that I will never be able to repay.

## What is the nature of your business and who do you serve?

I'm the founder and CEO of a media company called Matriarch Digital Media. It is a women-centered media company in Minnesota. We make on-demand content for women, primarily Gen X women. We started in the audio space, so I make podcasts and audio content as a part of a network and also for paying clients. Our business has one very specific goal. We are changing the way the world talks to and talks about women and girls. We start with women where they are in their lives. We are helping to change the language that they use to refer to themselves and we are helping to elevate their thinking because once they're thinking about themselves differently, the world around them will begin to match that. They will then hold the world around them to a higher standard.

## What would you say the after Kim effect is, or what has it had on your business?

As I said before, if Kim hadn't intervened when she did, I would not have a business. I was "this close" to closing it down within a matter of weeks, if not months. Kim made it so that I had the space to step back outside of the every day of my business and think about the bigger picture. She also gave me the space to think about myself as an entrepreneur and as a business person. She gave me the opportunity to do something that most people don't have a chance to do because they're just running too fast to do it. She gave me space to stop and think. She gave me space to stop and analyze *"Where I am in this? What role do I play? What am I holding on to that is difficult for me?"* And she gave me the safe space to not only go through those things, but also process and understand what is real in that story. What parts of the story I have clung to and used to beat myself up with to make it harder for me to do this. She helped me get out of my own way. When you're an entrepreneur and you are self-taught in all the things that you do, you constantly get in your own way. You're just afraid of messing it up. You're afraid of failing. You're afraid of making a mistake. She helped eliminate a lot of that thinking and gave me framework so that if I roll into that thinking, I can stop myself. I can say *"No, that's not what I do. No, that's not accurate to me. No, that is not what we talked about."* Being able to have those structures and systems in place means that when I struggle, I can go back to the structure we built. I can go back to the structure I know how to use. Let me be clear: She doesn't just show you how to create a structure. She basically shows you how to do the thinking so you can do that yourself in the future. The work she did with me in my core business has been work that I have been able to apply to my future business endeavors, offshoots of the business. I use it in the professional work that I do outside of my business. All of these things now come from an informed place where I know what my skill set is. Where I have confidence in the work that I do. Where I have an understanding of what I'm allowed to and entitled to ask for in terms of support I need for myself when I'm doing professional work. All of that comes back to Kim being so nurturing and so supportive when I was struggling. Now I don't have to struggle the same way that I did before. Being an entrepreneur is always going to be a challenge to an extent in that I'm still a Black woman out here trying to get money, but I'm a Black woman out here trying to get money with full confidence that I deserve that money. Now I have a plan of action and the ability to continue to build plans of action to do that. That happened because of Kim.

# Ask Yourself

- Do your organizational leaders have all stakeholder's best interest at heart? How do you know? What measurable indicators do you have that demonstrate this belief?
- How do you learn best? Are you able to utilize whatever processes that aid you in learning at work?
- In what ways is inequity evident at your place of work? Have these concerns been raised? Does your organization have processes in place that encourage raising those concerns? Do you feel safe using those processes?
- How diverse is your workplace across identities, i.e. gender, race, ethnicity, class, age, disability, sexuality, etc.? Are the concerns related to diversity addressed within your organization in ways to align with stated core values?
- Is work a welcoming and psychologically safe place for you?

# III. Know Thy Community

*"To ignore that a business is made up of folx who must share common goals that align to shared core values in order to achieve organizational outcomes continues to be a failing that many business leaders rarely overcome."*

*Kim Crayton*

# My Story

*"Let's be honest, the future of business is not out parents' workplace."*

*- Kim Crayton -*

I don't care how much of a subject matter expert you are, every effective educator knows that classroom management is the key to student success. The ability to create and enforce clear, consistent, and well-articulated roles, responsibilities, and boundaries helps ensure that all members of this community understand, even if they don't always agree, what behaviors are acceptable and how people will be held accountable for breaking those rules. There is immense benefit in creating boundaries at the onset of building relationships, both professional and personal. The complexity of creating those boundaries increases with efforts to renegotiate those relationships later on, which can lead to pushback with things like inclusion efforts. Unfortunately, many in society see "rules and boundaries" as something negative, as an attack against their personal "freedoms," but anyone who's considered to have excellent classroom management skills understands that without "rules and boundaries," no one feels truly safe. "Rules and boundaries" allow community members to seek safety and comfort in the predictable. When so much of our everyday encounters are unknown and often chaotic, "rules and boundaries" let folx know where they stand while providing safe spaces for growth. Through adopting "rules and boundaries," my students learned that I was a safe adult to share their most intimate and personal stories. They knew what information would be kept between us and what, by law as a mandated reporter, I had to share with others. They knew that holding them accountable when they violated our agreed-upon community boundaries didn't mean that I thought they were a "bad person" but that doing so ensured that all felt safe.

Developing an effective classroom management strategy was also when I first adopted an "impact over intention" and "equity over equality" perspective, although I wouldn't know how important such a shift in perspective would become to the success of my future work. As a certified special needs educator, my entire job was identifying areas in which each of my students faced academic and life-skill challenges and developing strategies that would help them meet their annual goals. Everything about my role was evaluating individual ability against stated outcomes and finding ways to assist in their growth. Focused, tailored, differentiated instruction was required. I would never use the individual education plan of a student with processing issues like ADHD or dyslexia on a student with a mild or moderate cognitive disability like Down syndrome and expect the same results, but this is exactly how we treat our community members. We have nurtured a culture that applies the standards of the status quo to everyone, which privileges those for whom the status quo was designed to support while targeting those for whom the status quo was intended to exclude and harm. Very little about our lived experiences exist within the binary, yet much of our worldview and expectations are approached by design from such a narrow and restricting lens. I didn't know it at the time but spending all that time with my students and their families uniquely prepared me for a life as a business strategist whose work is rooted in prioritizing the most vulnerable.

# My Truths

I love this work; the teaching, training, and advising. Seeing folx, particularly from underrepresented and marginalized communities, entering organizations where they feel comfortable enough to give back by sharing their knowledge enables the company to grow, innovate, differentiate, compete, and profit. I get so excited seeing my clients overcome their challenges to build organizations that allow them to survive a global pandemic while addressing the impact of the "racial reckoning." To see a team of all white folx develop the skills to do the work and ask questions regarding their impact and the potential for harming others. To question whether this decision or that act aligned with their core values. It's been such a refreshing experience to witness. Like most leadership teams, they had core values, but they were little more than words on the website. They weren't operationalized; they weren't used to develop the needed processes, procedures, and policies. They didn't know how to use those core values to measure progress, nor did they use them to base their decisions on. What's funny is that it's this shit that gets me off; I love taking abstract values and turning them into something that can be used to guide organizational decisions and behavior.

I'm also great at it. I'm sure this is due to my classroom management experience with managing conflict, de-escalating potential crisis-management issues both personally and professionally. I have a knack for tapping into the heart of conflict and getting to the honest moments where the pain resides in a situation. That work is hard and raw because it requires me to subordinate my immediate fears to channel the calm that these situations need to get to a resolution that seeks to stop the harm and make the injured parties whole.

As a teacher, I always had the "worst" students around me. The students that other teachers couldn't stand. They called me "Momma Crayton." I loved those kids, and they loved me. Some are still in my life, and their accounts of how our relationship shaped their adulthoods humble me. I was also that teacher that if you were too quiet, I would strategically build a relationship with you to find out what the hell was going on in your head. I know my brain doesn't stop, so I needed to know what the fuck you're thinking about because if something's about to pop off, I need you to let me know so I can get the hell out of here. For many, it was the first time a teacher took the time to get to know them because, as many teachers will tell you, most of our time is taken up by the disruptive or "gifted" students and the "average" student, who doesn't "cause problems" or isn't considered "special" just gets ignored. Taking the time to get to know these students helped me understand how vulnerable they were and that I had to prioritize their needs because they either wouldn't or didn't know how. It's the same within organizations. We pour all our attention into those folx that we deem "rock stars" while ignoring those members of the community who also add value. In my experience, these ignored and under-valued individuals are essential to a thriving business. The lived experiences of the most vulnerable enable organizational leaders to solve problems while minimizing harm.

# Our Truths

There is no such thing as equality within current systems, institutions, and policies; "desegregation" is proof of this. Desegregation was a failed experiment because accepting "Blackness" was never a part of the agreement. Desegregation required assimilation, a mandate that Black folx in white spaces shed or hide their "Blackness" and adopt a cloak of "whiteness" without assuming its benefits. As long as the folx with power and privilege are the only ones making decisions about how everyone else lives, "equality" is not a thing. Equity, on the other hand, is what's key to ensuring that folx from diverse backgrounds have similar experiences. We can never recreate the same experiences due to the inherent exclusionary and harmful nature of white supremacy and anti-Blackness. This is why I don't believe in empathy. There is no way a white cis, heterosexual Christian married man will ever "understand" what it is like to be in my shoes, nor I, his. So, asking the most vulnerable to wait around; to assume positive intent while the most powerful and privileged gain "the ability to identify with or understand another's situation or feelings" is bullshit. I shouldn't have to wait for someone else to "feel my pain" to want or expect them to stop harming me. Instead of championing nonexistent empathy, I encourage folx to sympathize and to extend compassion and grace, which only require an acknowledgment of a different lived experience. There's no need for me to "understand" someone else's lived experience to acknowledge the impact.

In the workplace, there are many situations that we incorrectly approach as "among equals" rather than "equity," and it is our failure to make this shift that continues to cause unmeasured harm. Two examples are what many call "microaggression," and the other is salary negotiation. A microaggression is "a comment or action that subtly and often unconsciously or unintentionally expresses a prejudiced attitude toward a member of a marginalized group (such as a racial minority)." I call this behavior what it is; what its impact is—**professional violence**—because there's nothing "micro" about the impact of this behavior. I define professional violence as any "intense, turbulent, or furious and often destructive action or force" in a professional situation that leverages the systems, institutions, and policies of white supremacy against a marginalized group member. As a Black woman who supervises whiteness, I should not have to spend an hour writing a damn email to provide information or let you know of an error in your work product. There is nothing "equal" about my having to craft my message in such a way that it doesn't trigger your emotions, particularly since Black women aren't given the space to express the full range of their emotions in professional settings. I should be able to say what I need to, and you take the damn feedback. The minute you decide to cry or lash out, now we're no longer addressing the email. I'm now put on the defensive while also being expected to manage your feelings. For example, crying to escape accountability is white women's super-power, and your tears are violent. Globally, white women's tears have resulted in the death of its target, and the fact that it's strategic is vile. If I have not hit you in your damn throat, your tears are not my concern. I have heard too many white women say when they get pulled over by the cops, they turn that shit on, enabling them to cast themselves as the victim rather than the villain.

Salary negotiation is another business task treated as an equality issue instead of an equity issue, which can hurt people in the long run. Most organizational processes don't look at or talk about the power dynamics between an employer and a [potential] employee, especially during "negotiations." Even though employment contracts are "negotiated" between unequal parties–an organization's legal department and someone trying to make an excellent first impression–the fact that "equality" is the default position is still a barrier. We gaslight the most vulnerable party in the "negotiation" with "You don't get what you don't ask for" as if asking is the only hurdle, instead of acknowledging that every negotiation is about leveraging the power and information dynamics the most vulnerable can't access professionally. Even as current salary transparency laws are being enacted, we are seeing how the powerful and privileged are using information asymmetry to leverage systems, institutions, and policies designed to exclude to get around the "intent" of such legislation.

# Common Myths

There's a myth that I'm constantly pushing against: Just because we spend time together, we're a community. Coming from a similar background or affinity group doesn't make a community. Community is a sense of belonging; it's something that is nurtured and taken care of; it grows or dies, it's a living thing, and it takes a commitment to the work of tending to that nurturing and growth. I have years of experience building and managing communities of all kinds. For instance, as a classroom teacher, I understood the importance of building trust so that my students felt safe enough to test their limitations while developing the skills needed to navigate the complexities of human relationships. So, this was on my mind when I decided to launch my #causeascene Discord server, Kim Crayton's Community Cafe, in response to the lack of support people were receiving from organizational leaders after the January 6, 2021, riot. To process their feelings ahead of the inauguration, I knew that ensuring a safe and welcoming experience was mandatory.

I had to think about the hours of operation. Since most people were used to the platform being "always open," I knew I didn't have the time or desire to watch that space around the clock, so I limited it to times when I knew someone would be there to help if needed. This was a decision that folx didn't understand initially but saw the value in action. Because I always wanted someone around when the server was opened, I made sure I had moderators. I even created a training they had to take to ensure that they were prepared to manage the space in a manner that maintained the community's trust. In addition to having trained moderators who could handle any potential concerns, from facilitating discussions to handling code of conduct violations, we also utilized bots that helped us practice using inclusive language. Building a healthy community is a lot of work. It is like deciding to have a great yard. Everybody wants a great-looking yard, but very few want or can do all the work needed to achieve it. There is a big difference between paying someone to put grass down, cutting, fertilizing, and weeding the yard versus doing it yourself. Whether you pay someone or do it yourself, each requires a different approach, but the goal of having a great yard is met.

Another thing many folx who create products and services get wrong is waiting to focus their attention on building and nurturing their community of stakeholders. They expend so much time, talent, and resources on getting to that MVP (minimal viable product) that many put off or ignore the communal nature of building the business, the policies, procedures, and processes way too long. Ideally, it would be best if you built your community while you develop and test your product and services; it needs to go hand and hand so you are not playing catch-up because once it grows, it's harder to go back to address those issues and concerns. **Reminder: It's much easier to establish appropriate boundaries, to hold folx accountable for their behavior at the start of a relationship versus renegotiating them later.**

A product or service is not a business; it's just a product or service, and this is where I've seen many of my clients get stuck. You're building a business once you move beyond the minutiae of a functioning product or service to operationalizing your core values into policies, procedures, and processes and enlisting the support of stakeholders. Once your focus shifts from internal [unknown] to external [known] is when you should shift to prioritize building community.

I met this guy at a conference in Berlin. He had written a popular programming language, "gave the code away," and was now working on a new language. I thought this would be a great way to try out different ways to build a community alongside developing an open-source product. Still, he did not see the need because all he wanted to think about was the code base, even though he'd shared with me that he was already experiencing problematic behavior among the individual contributors who had already signed on to help. He saw the value in what I was saying but couldn't see how it connected with his code. He kept saying, *"This is just a product. I don't know how successful it's going to be,"* and that's the problem. Waiting to build community or to see if what you're building is "going to work" after you've engaged stakeholders sets the stage for problematic and potentially harmful practices and behaviors to become the norm, especially if those early stakeholders don't have a wide range of perspectives and lived experiences. You need to think about building your community of stakeholders as you develop your products and services because they help inform those decisions. When it comes to building community, folx think it's "either-or." No, it's "both." Your stakeholders help inform your products and services and help build and run the business. This is why diversity matters in a knowledge economy; your product or service and business benefit from diverse perspectives and lived experiences. Without a diverse community of stakeholders to help guide your decisions, you'll miss out on opportunities that benefit the business and the ability to forecast and mitigate potential harm.

## Becoming the Antiracist Economist

### EARLY 2018:

- Started #causeascene: The Strategic Disruption of the Status Quo in Technical Organizations, Communities, and Events
- *Saving Capitalism* – Robert Reich, which introduced me to the Powell Memo [Netflix]
- *The Powell Memo*: Written in 1971 to the U.S. Chamber of Commerce, the Lewis Powell Memo was a blueprint for corporate domination of American Democracy. (See Appendix 1)
- *Requiem for the American Dream* – Noam Chomsky [Prime]
- *The Gilded Age* – PBS's American Experience
- *Poverty Inc.* [Prime]
- *Seeing White* series on the Scene On Radio Podcast
- *Stamped From the Beginning* – Ibram Kendi
- *The Family* [Netflix]
- *The Trilateral Commission: The Crisis of Democracy*
- *The Wealth of Nations* – Adam Smith [Considered the Grandfather of Economics]
- *The Real Adam Smith: Morality and Markets* [Prime]
- *The Real Adam Smith: Ideas that Changed the World* [Prime]
- *America & Mr. Smith* [Prime]

### THEMES I NEEDED TO UNPACK:

- Antiracist anti-capitalism
- Global profiting off anti-Blackness
- Whiteness can no longer remain unexamined.
- Call a thing a thing.

- Fundamental antiracist presidential policy agenda
- Equality vs. Equity
- Prioritizing the most vulnerable
- Focus on minimizing harm.
- Whiteness as hero or victim but never the villain
- Addressing our own internalized white supremacy and anti-Blackness
- I'm educating the "oppressor" while also processing my own oppression.
- White supremacy is the parasite that is now eating its host.
- The model minority myth
- "Definitions belong to the definers, not the defined."
- The Powell Memo is a blueprint for "antiracist capitalism."

## Questions I Asked Myself:

- Can any "definition" of capitalism/economy developed by whiteness ever be antiracist?
- Can economics be "moral"?
- What happens to an economy when its division of labor is consolidated i.e., from many people doing many specialized steps to few people or machines doing many, if not all, the steps?
- Does Adam Smith define who the "opportunity for everyone" includes?
- Does Adam Smith define who he considers to be "the least among us"?
- Does this include women? Slaves? The poor? Which poor?

- Can individual interest be pursued efficiently and effectively while minimizing harm and benefitting society as a whole?
- Can "self-love," which benefits "the self," function as a motivating factor for minimizing harm to others?
- How do you shift from an understanding of "labor" as a physical undertaking (Industrial Age) to an intellectual undertaking (Knowledge Age), which requires inclusion and diversity for business leaders to leverage as an asset that creates value?
- Who gets to determine what is "just"; "fair"?
- Who did Adam Smith see as the "average human being"?
- Who did Adam Smith not see as the "average human being"?
- It appears that all is here to create a "just" economic system if only "the average human being" is inclusive. Would this take a simple reimaging?
- What has "company as government" looked like throughout history?
- What does "company as government" look like today?
- What modern examples do we have of unprofitable companies that create wealth for founders and investors?
- How does the historical fact that Britain tried to extract wealth from "America" while making sure that no wealth went from Britain to "America" parallel current movements within marginalized communities against the economically and politically privileged?
- What does the division of labor look like in the 21st-century "just" economy?
- How has becoming a knowledge economy impacted the specialization theory when physical labor is no longer the dominant value indicator?
- What is "universal opulence to all ranks of people"? Who did Adam Smith include in identifying "all

ranks" and who did he exclude and how intentional was the exclusion?

- Adam Smith was very suspicious of cronyism "partnerships between government and business" i.e., lobbying. How can these relationships be effectively addressed today in our effort toward a "just" economy?
- What is an "economic democracy"?
- Can there be a "fair, open, fast, and trusted marketplace" for all?
- Does the ability for a marketplace to self-regulate change related to the selling of products/goods vs. services? Example: eBay vs Fivver
- What are examples of the U.S. extracting wealth without reciprocity?
- What incentives can be used to encourage an antiracist economy?
- How does one interact with the economy when the government, at every level, is actually creating the negative externalities that they're tasked with guarding against?

## Late 2018:

- Redefining Capitalism Without White Supremacy: The Economics of Being Antiracist
- Research Question: Can we create a world where economic privatization and public political systems prioritize the collective well-being?

## Gave my first talk on the subject at BITCON [Black In Technology Conference]

My goal: To help business leaders disrupt, innovate, and gain competitive advantage within the global marketplace while identifying and minimizing harm

## ADAM SMITH: THE FATHER OF ECONOMICS, THE WEALTH OF NATIONS, 1776

- "All for ourselves, and nothing for other people, seems, in every age of the world, to have been the vile maxim of the masters of mankind."
- "Consumption is the sole end and purpose of all production; and the interest of the producer ought to be attended to, only so far as it may be necessary for promoting that of the consumer."
- "What improves the circumstances of the greater part can never be regarded as an inconvenience to the whole. No society can surely be flourishing and happy, of which the far greater part of the members are poor and miserable."

## JAMES MADISON: THE CONSTITUTIONAL CONVENTION, 1787

- "The major concern of the society has to be to protect the minority of the opulent against the majority."

Why is this conversation about the economics of white supremacy important?

1. As an increasingly global community, we continue to view the world through the perspective/lens of WHITENESS, white supremacy, and ANTI-BLACKNESS.

2. Gaining this understanding helps to explain why current efforts for improving inclusion while minimizing harm just aren't working.
3. We must be willing to accept and deal with the truth that the "better us" we are working toward has NEVER been an option for large portions of the population.
4. To do better, those who benefit from the economics of white supremacy must be willing to prioritize the needs and safety of the most vulnerable in our communities in order that we all benefit from the collective brilliance of organizations that are able to innovate, differentiate, and gain and maintain competitive advantage.

## 2020

- I've been thinking about building this business school and the phrase "Profit Without Oppression" (PWO) kept repeating in my head. So, I bought the domain for inspiration: ProfitWithoutOppression.com
- I get to rethink education at scale.
- Great education shouldn't be the sole domain of the powerful and privileged.
- I've been researching and working with clients and the community for years to develop a business development approach that leverages welcoming and psychological safety for innovation and competitive advantage.
- #causeascene mattered when I still believed that systems, institutions, and policies designed to privilege the few at the expense of the many could be changed or dismantled. I now am committed to no longer putting new wine into old wineskins because I no longer believe that anything

DESIGNED to harm can be retrofitted to prioritize mini-mizing harm.

- #causeascene was angry, unsustainable and Profit Without Oppression is hopeful.
- While some choose to focus on the present, others like myself have chosen to build the future we want to experience.
- Instead of mixing capitalism with social change, what about shifting the lens to capitalism AS social change? In today's political and economic climate, it is more important than ever that we rethink how we scale, evolve, and recover our businesses, while also thinking deeply about our collective impact on society. Profit Without Oppression is that new lens.
- Community members will be introduced to a develop-ing theory that challenges the popular "capitalism is evil" perspective by reimagining a world where private enter-prise aligns with harm reduction and prioritizes the most vulnerable.

## Designing A Path Forward:

- Organizational leaders worldwide have been looking for an off-ramp that enables them to operate outside the clas-sic framing that "business as usual" requires adopting a PROFIT ONLY at all costs perspective.
- PWO provides anyone who seeks an entrepreneurial path to take an idea and build something that at its core pri-oritizes a supremacy-, coercion-, discrimination-, and exploitation-FREE stakeholder impact.

- Organizational development that's rooted in prioritizing minimizing harm and the most vulnerable should be approached as community development.
- This is NOT a system to be implemented; it's a lens through which one makes decisions and guides behavior.
- This is not a magic bullet and it's hard work.
- This is not a one-size-fits-all solution; it is an organizational orientation.
- PWO is the lens through which you view the business landscape...every resource, relationship, and responsibility.
- The tenets of PWO can be applied to public, private, non-profit, for-profit, and governmental entities.
- Building a team with the "right" folx is one thing; getting those individuals to work together in ways that are strategic, innovative, competitive, collaborative, and profitable is quite another. Getting your team to value collaboration and to share what they know/learn with others ensures that organizational leaders are able to leverage the knowledge and skills they need to make decisions that matter in furthering their PWO initiatives.
- In a PWO ecosystem, the stock market is not the only indicator of the economy's health; it's not even the most important.
- Those who undertake establishing a PWO ethos must understand that any form of oppression, discrimination, and harm is amplified when they intersect anti-Blackness and must plan to mitigate the impact.
- PWO is a blueprint toward an antiracist economy.
- What we need to be talking about is what does PROFIT look like if we challenge every touch point in bringing products/services to market that oppress or have the potential to oppress.

Every part of our current political, social, and economic systems, institutions, and policies are rooted in oppression. They require domination, theft, dishonesty, discrimination, and the harming of others as fuel to operate AND are designed to discourage, and even crush, any challenge.

Then there are those who understand that this is not only unethical and immoral, but that it is also unsustainable. The flaws that inherently exist when exclusion is the business model are increasingly being highlighted on a global scale.

## What is needed is a community of folx

- who are no longer willing to put new wine into old wineskins.
- who fundamentally understand that "We get there together or not at all."
- who want to be a part of the process of defining a common, inclusive language and address some of the barriers that currently exist related to business models, legal concerns, and funding.
- who believe that our ONLY choices aren't business vs. social change and are forging a path toward business AS social change.

## What's the Difference Between Traditional vs. Profit Without Oppression Business Models?

## TRADITIONAL BUSINESS MODELS:

1. Product/Service (P/S) first mindset
2. P/S dictates organizational operations
3. Scale at all costs

4. Shareholder-value ONLY consideration
5. P/S development guides decisions related to any core values

## PROS:

1. Tightly focused [attention; get to X (i.e # of sales/customers/units, IPO, etc)]
2. Binary decision-making
3. Status quo; familiar
4. More easily resourced

## CONS:

1. Benefits the already powerful and privileged
2. Increased potential for crisis event/s
3. Shareholder ONLY focused harms; creates unintended risk, and increasingly crisis-management issues
4. Replicates systems, institutions, and policies (S/I/P) designed to exclude and harm
5. Efforts to minimize harm are often unsuccessful due to S/I/P that, by design, can't accommodate such initiatives i.e. DEI, codes of conduct, inclusive language, etc.
6. Inability to forecast and mitigate potential harm
7. P/S dependent
8. Market conditions have a greater influence and impact due to P/S ONLY focus
9. P/S ONLY focused means that all eggs are in one basket, which influences and impacts decision-making.
10. P/S ONLY means that everything that leads to increasing shareholder value is a potential option [rudderless; goes wherever the wind blows]

## Profit Without Oppression Business Models:

1. Human-centric first mindset
2. Core values dictate operations
3. Supremacy-, coercion-, discrimination-, and exploitation-FREE is the foundation
4. Stakeholder value-focused
5. Core values guide decisions related to P/S development
6. Operations over P/S

## PROS:

1. Considers stakeholder impact
2. Risk-management strategy that prioritizes harm reduction
3. Decreased potential for crisis event/s
4. Provides alternatives to S/I/P deigned to exclude and harm
5. Leverages lived experiences, particularly those from marginalized and vulnerable communities
6. Makes "No" easier ["Does this align with core values?"]
7. Permission to chart a new course; true innovation
8. Improved ability to forecast and mitigate potential harm
9. Not P/S dependent
10. Facilitates Organizational Hospitality

## CONS:

1. Takes longer to stand up
2. Has to consider and resolve P/S with stakeholder impact [a more complex decision-making process; can be uncomfortable and messy]
3. Few examples to follow
4. Harder to get resourced

5.  Knowing that harm can only be minimized and
    not eliminated

## What does PWO look like in the workplace?

- Making sure that marginalized communities within the
  larger organizational community are not pitted against
  each other for attention and/or resources
- An understanding that organizations are NOT families...
  this is manipulative
- Compensation structure = baseline + # of roles
  and responsibilities
- An understanding that white women are not diversity
- An understanding of the harm inflicted when whiteness
  enters marginalized spaces
- Understands that all speech/opinions/perspectives are
  not equal
- Understands the myth of "The Culture Wars"
- Prioritizes impact over intention
- Welcoming and psychological safety
- Lived experience over theory
- Authentic conversations
- Hopefulness
- Strategic action
- "Kind" over "nice"
- Community health over individual contribution
- Equity over equality
- Hiring for lived experiences
- Understands that the ethos of "move fast and break
  things" is problematic because leadership rarely stops to
  ask: What did we break, how did we break it, who did we
  harm, and how do we make amends?

- Has stopped looking for simple solutions to complex problems
- Understands the differences between instant gratification vs. long-term strategy
- Understands that collaboration cannot be forced; it must be encouraged by removing barriers and building trust
- Understands that they must invest in transitioning domain expert to managing the roles and responsibilities of others
- Understands the "soft skills" myth and how it undermines efforts to maintain welcoming and psychological safety
- Understands that the lack of diversity within their industry/organization is not a pipeline issue
- Understands that the roles and responsibilities of DEI = HR and should be removed from the operations vertical because their mandates don't align and placed under the CEO

## EXAMPLE 1:

There's a common, problematic "understanding" that thrives in startup culture regarding COOs, which has hampered many from moving beyond scalable product/service to an efficient and effective business:

1. That they aren't essential
2. They're only needed at scale
3. This role should be automated ASAP
4. This role is subordinate to CEO & CTO

Appropriate perspective:

- CEO & COO are opposite sides of the same coin
- The CEO is the external facing role; the vision

- The COO is the internal facing role; the operations

## EXAMPLE 2:

One area where we face challenges when attempting to address supremacy in the workplace is related to organizational hierarchy. Our attempts in the past, flat orgs, no titles, etc., have led to chaotic situations with folx not knowing how to hold each other accountable for outcomes. Here's an approach that I've developed:

### PERSON + ROLE [WE FUNCTION IN "ROLES"]

- Person in the role of leader rather than "leader"
- Person in the role of manager rather than "manager"
- Person in the role of coder, researcher, assistant, scientist, analyst, etc.
- My "boss" vs. the person who manages my roles and responsibilities [It's the difference between who one is vs. what one does.] This distinction is important because we behave differently when we believe someone is challenging "who we are" vs. "what we do."
- There is never a "boss," only those who are tasked with managing the roles and responsibilities of others.
- Example [all aligned to organizational core values]:
  - Level 1: Role + responsibilities
  - Level 2: Manages the roles and responsibilities of Level 1
  - Level 3: Manages the roles and responsibilities of Level 2
  - Etc.
- So, a person in a role is tasked with managing "self" and levels, which means that you manage the responsibilities [tasks] of a role and not the "personality" of the individual in that role. Adopting this framework also facilitates

the ability to have a more equitable process for holding folx accountable for behaviors that fall outside their
assigned role/s and responsibilities.

# What You Need to Know

## Applicant selection

 **Kim Crayton ~ Antiracist Economist ~ She/Her** ●
@KimCrayton1

If your "diversity" consultant/expert is NOT forcing
you to redefine your idea of the PERFECT applicant
or employee and requiring you to become
uncomfortable, then you will NOT successful
recruit and staff from members of marginalized
communities

#causeascene

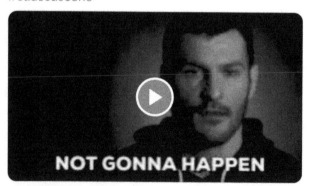

2:09PM · Oct 22, 2018 · Twitter for iPhone

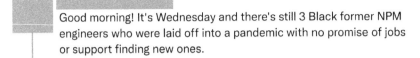

Good morning! It's Wednesday and there's still 3 Black former NPM engineers who were laid off into a pandemic with no promise of jobs or support finding new ones.

Why haven't you hired them yet? Yes, you.

Anyway you know what's cool? It's actually super common for white folks with friends at companies to basically bypass entire sections of interview processes or having them be ceremonial, but as soon as it's someone Black, everyone is VERY CONCERNED about "not lowering the bar".

 **Kim Crayton ~ Antiracist Economist ~ She/Her** 👏
@KimCrayton1

# PREACH 👏👏👏👏

# This is rooted in white supremacy and anti-Blackness and for EV. ER. Y. one of y'all white folx who's ever said or done anything to SUPPORT this discriminatory behavior, and that INCLUDES saying nothing as it was happening in your face, fuck you 🖕

> Jul 8
>
> Anyway you know what's cool? It's actually super common for white folks with friends at companies to basically bypass entire sections of interview processes or having them be ceremonial, but as soon as it's someone Black, everyone is VERY CONCERNED about "not lowering the bar".

11:20AM · Jul 8, 2020 · Twitter for iPhone

## Interview Process

 **Kim Crayton ~ Antiracist Economist ~ She/Her**
@KimCrayton1

A Lesson for Building a Learning Organization from "It Doesn't Have To Be Crazy At Work"

This is how to hire for an knowledge economy:

1. You acknowledge through pay that applicants time is valuable

2. The interview process is relevant

#causeascene

For example, when we're choosing a new designer, we hire each of the finalists for a week, pay them $1,500 for that time, and ask them to do a sample project for us. Then we have something to evaluate that's current, real, and completely theirs.

What we don't do are riddles, blackboard problem solving, or fake "come up with the answer on the spot" scenarios. We don't answer riddles all day, we do real work. So we give people real work to do and the appropriate time to do it in. It's the same kind of work they'd be doing if they got the job.

The idea 1

11:51AM · Aug 1, 2019 · Buffer

**Kim Crayton ~ Antiracist Economist ~ She/Her** 🌑
@KimCrayton1

New Study Shows Age, Race And Gender Bias In the Interview Process

#causeascene

A highlighted example pitted 28-year-old white men who possessed 9 years' of relevant experience competing against 50-year-old white and black men and women with 31 years' experience, researchers noted that the applications from young white men were:

- 1.8 times more likely to be selected for interview than ones from 50-year-old white men

- 2.3 times more likely to be selected than those from 50-year-old white women

- 2.6 times more likely to be selected than those from 50-year-old black men

- 3 times more likely to be selected than those from 50-year-old black women

2:03PM · May 4, 2019 · Buffer

## Offer Negotiation

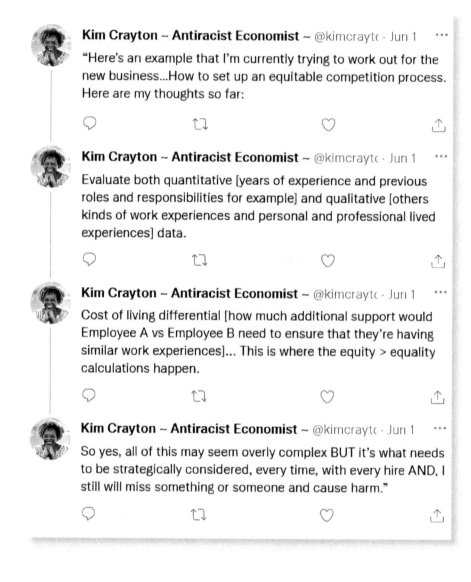

**Kim Crayton ~ Antiracist Economist** ~ @kimcrayto · Jun 1 ···

"Here's an example that I'm currently trying to work out for the new business...How to set up an equitable competition process. Here are my thoughts so far:

**Kim Crayton ~ Antiracist Economist** ~ @kimcrayto · Jun 1 ···

Evaluate both quantitative [years of experience and previous roles and responsibilities for example] and qualitative [others kinds of work experiences and personal and professional lived experiences] data.

**Kim Crayton ~ Antiracist Economist** ~ @kimcrayto · Jun 1 ···

Cost of living differential [how much additional support would Employee A vs Employee B need to ensure that they're having similar work experiences]... This is where the equity > equality calculations happen.

**Kim Crayton ~ Antiracist Economist** ~ @kimcrayto · Jun 1 ···

So yes, all of this may seem overly complex BUT it's what needs to be strategically considered, every time, with every hire AND, I still will miss something or someone and cause harm."

## Recruiting

 **Kim Crayton ~ Antiracist Economist ~ She/Her**
@KimCrayton1

The #1 thing to remember when recruiting, hiring, and retaining marginalized talent in tech...

MONEY MAY GET US IN THE BUT PSYCHOLOGICAL SAFETY WILL KEEP US FROM WALKING RIGHT BACK OUT

#causeascene

3:07PM · Oct 22, 2018 · Twitter for iPhone

## Knowledge Organizational Sharing[Explicit/Tacit]

**Kim Crayton ~ Antiracist Economist ~ She/Her** 🖤🤎
@KimCrayton1

When are tech leaders gonna learn that we're NOT making widgets anymore...this is a knowledge economy, which REQUIRES the strategic ability to share & scale organizational knowledge, which REQUIRES the fostering a culture of welcoming, collaboration & psychological safety

> ▓▓▓▓▓▓▓▓▓▓▓▓▓▓ Feb 18
>
> It turns out the Ethical AI team was the last to know about a massive reorganization, which was prompted by our advocacy. This was not communicated with us at all, despite promises that it would be.
>
> bloomberg.com/news/articles/...

3:53PM · Feb 18, 2021 · Twitter for iPhone

**Kim Crayton ~ Antiracist Economist ~ She/Her**
@KimCrayton1

Inclusion & diversity in tech won't improve w/o radical changes n hiring & culture. We require an interviewing process that seeks individuals w the ability to create, retain, & share tacit knowledge. We're no longer competing w widgets; we're competing w knowledge

#causeascene

> ▓▓▓▓▓▓▓▓▓ Jun 16
>
> I went through what felt like 500 rounds of interviews and test projects with Google - all the way to the on-site in Mountain View - and still didn't get the gig. even though I reportedly dazzled. so. that's all I got. I've been burnt out on tech as an industry for years now.

2:16AM · Jun 17, 2018 · Twitter for iPhone

## Joining HR/Legal

**Kim Crayton ~ Antiracist Economist ~ She/Her** ⬤... @KimCrayton1
Non-disparagement, and many confidentiality, agreements are legal
barriers to creating the welcoming and psychological safety we seek
in tech

I will NEVER sign an NDA and this is why I now include my CoC and a
clause in my contracts that I will NOT stay silent if...

> ▓▓▓▓▓▓▓▓▓ · May 2
>
> Hey @basecamp ▓▓▓▓▓▓▓ can you confirm whether or
> not the severance package you offered requires a NDA and/or
> non disparagement clause?

**Kim Crayton ~ Antiracist Economist ~ She/Her** ⬤
@KimCrayton1

1. I've advised leadership of potential harm, they
ignored me, harm was inflicted, AND no effort is
made to make amends

2. In the commission of my work, I DISCOVER that
harm was inflicted AND no effort is made to make
amends

Silencing criticism ensures we can't move forward

10:46AM · May 2, 2021 · Twitter for iPhone

## Onboarding

 **Kim Crayton ~ Antiracist Economist ~ She/Her**
@KimCrayton1

Onboarding is an essential part of any new hire/new community process, particularly for ensuring that members from underrepresented and marginalized groups feel welcomed, safe and supported

8:35PM · Jan 7, 2018 · Twitter for iPhone

## Retention

I think about this Angela Davis quote often..

"I have a hard time accepting diversity as a synonym for justice. Diversity...is a strategy designed to ensure that the institution functions in the same way it functioned before...It's a difference that doesn't make a difference."

 **Kim Crayton ~ Antiracist Economist ~ She/Her**
@KimCrayton1

This is why so many fail at it...diversity is only one part, recruitment

The real work is in inclusion, retention, which REQUIRES fundamental change that prioritizes the most vulnerable

4:49AM · Dec 16, 2019 · Twitter for iPhone

## DEI Removed from HR DEI = HR

**Kim Crayton ~ Antiracist Economist ~ She/Her**
@KimCrayton1

Here's my unpopular, yet honest assessment of current DEI "efforts"

If you can't stomach being paid to be gaslit, it's not the role for you

Here're some other warning signs:

1. This isn't a C-level role, that sits OUTSIDE of HR but under the CEO

HR & DEI are often at odds

· May 6

Personal news alert

Feb 4 was my last day as Director of Diversity, Equity, and Inclusion for @KQED. After some much-needed rest, reflection, and recovery from my time as KQEDs first Director of DEI, it's time for a ▮:

4:12PM · May 7, 2022 · Twitter for iPhone

**Kim Crayton ~ Antiracist Economist ~ She/Her** 🖤🕊️
@KimCrayton1

I've been talking about this for awhile now

HR's role and prioritizes, organizational risk/crisis
management, do NOT align with DEI's, relationship
management

HR should be housed under COO, operations,
& DEI under CEO, vision & both with the same level
of influence & support

> ▬▬▬▬ · Mar 14
> Why is every DEI role in tech under HR?
>
> That to me is a ⚑

11:03AM · Mar 14, 2022 · Twitter for iPhone

**Kim Crayton ~ Antiracist Economist ~ She/Her** ●... @KimCrayton1
Tech is NOT neutral nor apolitical AND here's an example for why I'm
an advocate of REMOVING any DEI efforts out of HR

Fundamentally, HR !== DEI

They're both vital for operationalizing and protecting org policies,
procedures, processes but "their clients" are NOT aligned

> The subjects of the report alleging
> discrimination point to examples such as
> "changing standards for promotions, unequal
> compensation, being set back in their careers
> after maternity leave, and experiencing
> retribution when they take their cases to HR."
> The report also detailed instances of alleged
> harassment and demotion after employees filed
> a complaint with Dropbox HR or returned to
> work following maternity leave.

**Kim Crayton ~ Antiracist Economist ~ She/Her** ●... @KimCrayton1
HR can't protect the organization's interest AND create welcoming
and psychological safety in our current business climate that ONLY
prioritizes shareholders OVER stakeholders

Just think about it...so many things that we know would help workers,
would harm current business models

**Kim Crayton ~ Antiracist Economist ~ She/Her** ●
@KimCrayton1

Ideally, DEI would be C-Level that has the
autonomy, resources & authority to advocate &
protect workers...and no I'm NOT talking about a
union because too many forward an white
supremacy & anti-Blackness agenda

DEI & HR would work together as equal
departments to resolve issues

1:25PM · Jul 28, 2021 · Twitter for iPhone

**Kim Crayton ~ Antiracist Economist ~ She/Her** 🤎... @KimCrayton1

I'll take this a step further because I believe ALL employee "advocacy" should be REMOVED from HR

HR, under COO, plays an important role in operationalizing and protecting the interests of the organization

> Jan 30
>
> People are always trying to figure out where to 'put' Talent Acquisition.
>
> Report to HR? Align with marketing?
>
> Here's a crazy idea: maybe it should be its own damn thing.
>
> Hiring people? Seems pretty important...

**Kim Crayton ~ Antiracist Economist ~ She/Her** 🤎
@KimCrayton1

Hiring, DEI, harassment complaints, etc should sit at the same level as HR under CEO as a "people/stakeholder role"

Folx tasked with these roles and responsibilities should have the equivalent authority, autonomy, and resources on par with HR

9:39AM · Jan 30, 2022 · Twitter for iPhone

# How to Have Effective and Efficient DEI Initiatives

1. Understand whether you're trying to turn around a canoe vs. a cruise ship: This is NOT about the size of the organization but an evaluation of the calcification of its culture. How ready are folx to do the real work?
2. Develop a systems thinking mindset. Know that your effort, great or small, will have a ripple effect throughout your "system" that will have immediate, short- and long-term, known and unknown impact and consequences.
3. Based on these factors, seek out and work to understand who's the most vulnerable and how are they being impacted.

   Side Note: To gain the most accurate data requires a commitment to establishing and nurturing welcoming and psychological safety as an organizational imperative.
4. Once this is understood, partner with them to develop a strategy tied to desired organizational benchmarks and outcomes, that's designed to address their concerns

without exacerbating harm, i.e. making them the targets of any resulting blowback.

5. Widely AND regularly communicate those organizational benchmarks and outcomes.

Strategy must be adopted organization-wide in policies, procedures, and processes.

6. Measure and hold folx at every level accountable, not just the DEI "department." Every effort should be made to turn your canoe or cruise ship around with minimal impact to those on board or in its "wake."

## CEO=COO

**Kim Crayton ~ Antiracist Economist ~ She/Her** 🖤🤍
@KimCrayton1

This is why I'm working on this talk now

"COO: The Most Disrespected Yet Necessary Role In Tech"

All to often the CEO is positioned as the valued but most have no idea how to operationalize "their great ideas"

#causeascene

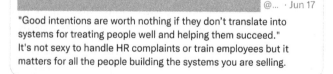

@... · Jun 17

"Good intentions are worth nothing if they don't translate into systems for treating people well and helping them succeed." It's not sexy to handle HR complaints or train employees but it matters for all the people building the systems you are selling.

2:54PM · Jun 17, 2019 · Twitter for iPhone

## Shareholder vs. Stakeholders

 **Kim Crayton ~ Antiracist Economist ~ She/Her**
@KimCrayton1

Diversity = Recruitment = Welcoming

Inclusion = Retention = Psychological Safety

Both are essential as we seek to shift from prioritizing shareholder ➡️ stakeholder value

Stakeholders are those who:

- Work for you
- Partner with you
- Buy from you
- Invest in you

5:36AM · Mar 8, 2021 · Twitter for iPhone

**Kim Crayton ~ Antiracist Economist ~ She/Her** 🖤🤍
@KimCrayton1

Our business practices/priorities:

Shareholder Value vs Stakeholder Value

are simply reflections of social norms/priorities:

Individualism vs Community

#TheFutureIsFREE & #ProfitWithoutOppression prioritizes Stakeholder Value, Community, minimizing harm & the most vulnerable

3:58AM · Jan 11, 2022 · Twitter for iPhone

## Evaluation

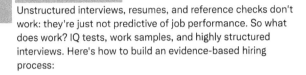

Unstructured interviews, resumes, and reference checks don't work: they're just not predictive of job performance. So what does work? IQ tests, work samples, and highly structured interviews. Here's how to build an evidence-based hiring process:

The Science Behind Making Software Engineering Interviews Truly Predictive of Job Performance ← Qualified

🔗 qualified.io

 **Kim Crayton ~ Antiracist Economist ~ She/Her** 🌐
@KimCrayton1

Yet again someone in tech who a large following, publicly expresses a harmful opinions

"Unstructured interviews are plagued by our own biases"

When are y'all gonna grasp that EVERYTHING is plagued with bias and our job is to acknowledge and mitigate its potential for harm

11:24AM · May 23, 2020 · Twitter Web App

Kim Crayton ~ Antiracist Economist ~ She/Her 🖤
@KimCrayton1

It's a slippery slope from your statements about bias to this mess

IQ tests have ALWAYS been used to gate-keep AND maintain the status quo

---

May 23

"You either accept my view that white people have higher IQs or its time for a race war" is a hell of a take, even from this shameless grifter.

wars.

Don't you get it yet?

Those who reject and attack IQ want the race wars.

14m

Replying to ▮▮▮▮▮▮

▮▮▮, I accept all the current understanding about IQ: its impact on

---

2:47PM · May 23, 2020 · Twitter Web App

## Mentoring

**Kim Crayton ~ Antiracist Economist ~ She/Her**
@kimcrayton1

"Positive mentoring relationships improves levels of engagement."

## Managing Your Feelings

**Kim Crayton ~ Antiracist Economist ~ She/Her**
@KimCrayton1

I don't care

These are my rules

Engage or not, your choice BUT my rules

I'm no longer responsible for the feelings of whiteness

We're full ass adults but ONLY one of us has an expectation of managing their feelings so the other feels comfortable

Feelings !== Actual Harm

6:15PM · Oct 21, 2019 · Twitter for iPhone

**Kim Crayton ~ Antiracist Economist ~ She/Her**
@KimCrayton1

YES

The days of me prioritizing and managing the
feelings of white folks is done

If you find me intimidating, angry, aggressive, etc,
know that I have historical cause to be and if I
haven't touched you, then take that shit up in your
next therapy session

#causeascene

7:24AM · Oct 3, 2019 · Twitter Web App

**Kim Crayton ~ Antiracist Economist ~ She/Her**
@KimCrayton1

Intention without strategy is CHAOS...

The cost of unmanaged "feelings" in the workplace
is high AND will no longer be the sole burden of the
most vulnerable

3:16PM · Apr 30, 2021 · Twitter Web App

## Giving and Receiving Feedback

 **Kim Crayton ~ Antiracist Economist ~ She/Her**
@KimCrayton1

#MentoringMinute giving and receiving feedback that's of value takes practice.

7:12AM · Nov 28, 2016 · Buffer

 **Kim Crayton ~ Antiracist Economist ~ She/Her** 
@KimCrayton1

#MentoringMinute When giving feedback, it helps if solutions are also provided.

7:12AM · Nov 29, 2016 · Buffer

## Training and Development

 **Kim Crayton ~ Antiracist Economist ~ She/Her** 
@KimCrayton1

PSA...the remedy for addressing the systems, institutions, and policies of white supremacy and anti-Blackness within your organization is NOT, let me repeat...is NOT training

These are NOT training issues

STOP LOOKING FOR SIMPLE SOLUTIONS TO COMPLEX PROBLEMS

10:25AM · May 20, 2021 · Twitter for iPhone

223

## Termination

 **Kim Crayton ~ Antiracist Economist ~ She/Her**
@KimCrayton1

Yep

The ability for privilege to win even when its behavior results in termination of employment has no equal

#causeascene

> Jan 24
>
> With all the layoffs happening, my mind keeps circling back to the fact that Megyn Kelly got $30 million in severance after defending blackface on national television.

11:28AM · Jan 24, 2019 · Twitter for iPhone

**Kim Crayton ~ Antiracist Economist ~ She/Her** 🌐
@KimCrayton1

This sounds about WHITE

Black folx get fired everyday for shit they didn't do, as regional manager, she was held accountable...move on because there's nothing new here...EXCEPT white folx being treated .01% like everyone else

#causeascene

 **NBC10 Philadelphia** ✓
@NBCPhiladelphia

A former manager is suing @Starbucks, claiming the company discriminated against her and other white employees while dealing with the aftermath of the controversial arrests of two black men at a Philadelphia store.

Starbucks Accused of Discriminating Against White Workers
nbcphiladelphia.com

6:40 AM · 10/31/19 · SocialFlow

6:08AM · Nov 1, 2019 · Buffer

**Kim Crayton ~ Antiracist Economist ~ She/Her** 🌍
@KimCrayton1

"Google could have fired Mr. Rubin and paid him little to nothing on the way out. Instead, the company handed him a $90 million exit package."

LACK OF INCLUSION IS A RISK MANAGEMENT ISSUE

#causeascene

Andy Rubin, the creator of Android, left Google in 2014 with a $90 million exit package. The last payment is scheduled for next month. Tomohiro Ohsumi/Bloomberg

## *How Google Protected Andy Rubin, the 'Father of Android'*

The internet giant paid Mr. Rubin $90 million and praised him, while keeping silent about a misconduct claim.

6:20PM · Oct 25, 2018 · Crowdfire Inc.

226

**Kim Crayton ~ Antiracist Economist ~ She/Her** ⬤... @KimCrayton1
So I wanna dive into @nhannahjones not receiving tenure because too many of you are missing it

Folx, particularly white academics, if you can't see that this moment is bigger than this one decision, then you haven't been paying attention, which is apart of the problem

**Kim Crayton ~ Antiracist Economist ~ She/Her** ⬤
@KimCrayton1

@UNC, like @Google when they fired @timnitGebru, has enabled folx with an inability to manage their feelings to create an unnecessary and under-calculated crisis management issue

Because here again, Black women have evidence that, checking ALL the boxes doesn't matter

6:00AM · May 20, 2021 · Twitter for iPhone

**Kim Crayton ~ Antiracist Economist ~ She/Her** ⬤
@KimCrayton1

To say that someone, at such a high level, was fired because their behavior was not aligned with the company's values, suggests to me that those values may not be as ingrained in the culture as some may think.

2:53PM · Feb 21, 2018 · Twitter for iPhone

**Kim Crayton ~ Antiracist Economist ~ She/Her**
@KimCrayton1

## DEAR BUSINESS LEADERS,

Warning signs that u need a risk management strategy & potential legal representation

- Ur employees r being harassed online n the commission of their duties
- Their off work activity includes calling out discrimination & they've been fired

#causeascene

11:34PM · Jul 10, 2018 · Twitter for iPhone

**Kim Crayton ~ Antiracist Economist ~ She/Her** 🌑
@KimCrayton1

"Legendary BBC broadcaster fired for tweeting picture of chimpanzee as royal baby"

So no, white supremacy and racism are not uniquely U.S. phenomenas

WHERE THERE'S WHITENESS, THERE'S ANTI-BLACKNESS

#causeascene

A BBC broadcaster has been fired after tweeting a joke about Prince Harry and Meghan Markle's newborn baby using a photograph of a chimpanzee.

Danny Baker, a veteran broadcaster and journalist in the U.K., earlier apologized for his "stupid unthinking gag," which he claimed was not meant to have any racist undertones.

"This was a serious error of judgment and goes against the values we as a station aim to embody," a BBC spokesman said in a statement. "Danny's a brilliant broadcaster but will no longer be presenting a weekly show with us."

6:08AM · May 9, 2019 · Buffer

## Resignation

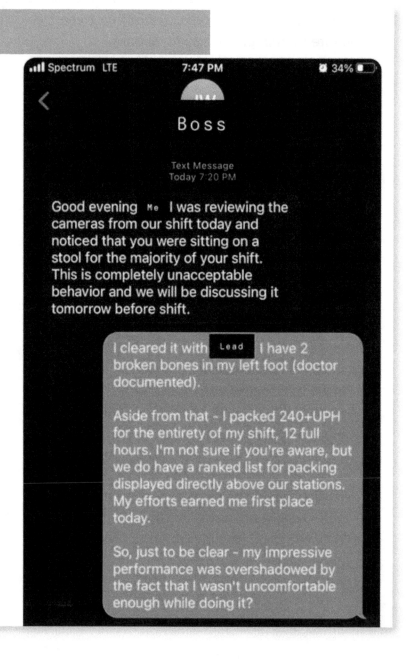

I'm really not appreciating your attitude. You could have just said the first part where it was cleared with another lead instead of being disrespectful. This type of behavior isn't going to get you anywhere here.

Hey, thanks for wasting my precious off time with some garbage you didn't bother to investigate beforehand.

Seriously - 240+ UPH - what you claim to be the pinnacle of performance there, I achieved it, and I get grief because I was sitting while doing it. You guys need to get your priorities straight. It is no wonder that you have such difficulties retaining staff.

I'm not concerned with going "anywhere" there. It's a toxic environment with ignorant people at the helm. I won't be in tomorrow or ever again.

We don't need to rush to you leaving. Let's talk in the morning and we can sort this out.

No thanks. Have a good life.

**Kim Crayton ~ Antiracist Economist ~ She/Her** 🏿
@KimCrayton1

Unmanaged feelings in the workplace is the LARGEST untracked detriment to morale, productivity, and retention

This is why there's a GREAT RESIGNATION...folx are trying to survive a fuckin pandemic and putting up with professional violence is NO LONGER AN OPTION

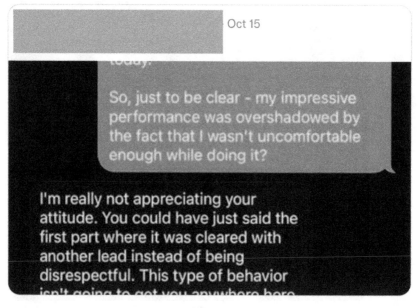

11:08AM · Oct 21, 2021 · Twitter for iPhone

**Kim Crayton ~ Antiracist Economist ~ She/Her** 🖐
@KimCrayton1

All of this...your idea of the "Great Resignation", particularly when related to the historically marginalized and vulnerable, is actually these folx recognizing their economic value of the knowledge, skills, and BODIES and leveraging this insight to their benefit

Oct 20

Labeling attrition as the "Great Resignation" is a cop out from ACTUALLY interrogating toxic & unhealthy workplace culture, structure & lack of growth mobility.

Especially when attrition keeps happening at junior levels and with BIPOC staff. It's a great LOSS.

10:29AM · Oct 20, 2021 · Twitter for iPhone

## Exiting HR/Legal, i.e., NDAs

**Kim Crayton ~ Antiracist Economist ~ She/Her**
@KimCrayton1

So it seems that @GatsbyJS is yet another tech company that can't get diversity and inclusion right BUT has at the ready an NDA to silence those very same voices from speaking publicly

If you're serious about listening and learning [redacted], release everyone from these

> [redacted] Aug 17
> Hey [redacted] I can think of one thing you can do for those silenced "marginalized voices"

3:27PM · Aug 17, 2020 · Twitter Web App

**Kim Crayton ~ Antiracist Economist ~ She/Her** ... @KimCrayton1
So, I'm watching ep 2 of the new #SurvivingRKelly series and I'm half way in ONLY to discover that there's a 3rd white woman [an attorney], the first were a pair of sisters from ep 1 who worked for him, who actively facilitate/d this abuse of Black women and girls

 **Kim Crayton ~ Antiracist Economist ~ She/Her** ... @KimCrayton1
White women have a long history of not only maintaining and promoting white supremacy by supporting white men but also by aiding Black men in harming Black women and girls.

White women can be fucking a Black man, while denigrating every Black woman in his life

 **Kim Crayton ~ Antiracist Economist ~ She/Her**
@KimCrayton1

"Loggans began what I can a sort of settlement factory. Girls would come to her with charges of underage sexual contact with Kelly. She would send them to a private detective agency...make them take a lie detector test. A settlement would be struck, a NDA would be signed...

7:29AM · Jan 5, 2020 · Twitter for iPhone

235

**Kim Crayton ~ Antiracist Economist ~ She/Her**
@KimCrayton1

So, I have the energy for this today

There are ONLY 2 responses I/we needed from you on this issue @anildash:

1. Yes. Meaning that the NDA portion of any severance agreements are now null and void for ALL previous employees, including from 18 months ago

2. No.

> **Kim Crayton ~ Antiracist Economist ~ She/Her** @KimCra... · May 29
>
> There's so much I want to say in response to this thread and yet my community is on fire and I just don't have the energy for you
>
> I'll leave you with what I'm hearing from others in the community...WE EXPECTED BETTER FROM YOU!

8:18AM · Jun 4, 2020 · Twitter Web App

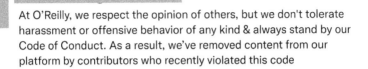

At O'Reilly, we respect the opinion of others, but we don't tolerate harassment or offensive behavior of any kind & always stand by our Code of Conduct. As a result, we've removed content from our platform by contributors who recently violated this code

**Kim Crayton ~ Antiracist Economist ~ She/Her** 🌍… @KimCrayton1
This is great and yet as I communicated to @pluralsight, not naming the thing causes confusion and pushes the emotional burden of education onto the most vulnerable in our communities

Kim is right about this. If you're taking action to protect the people who have been harmed, those people deserve to know that these consequences happened.

It removes some of the accountability when you don't include the information. He publicly harassed and bullied people on here - he shouldn't benefit from the protection of his consequences being hidden.

**Kim Crayton ~ Antiracist Economist ~ She/Her** 🌍
@KimCrayton1

Oh yeah, I'm sick of orgs covering their asses when individuals they've associated w cause harm

I've seen to many orgs that don't have job descriptions or any effect process for collecting and analyzing data but they'll hand you an NDA 1st day

But don't worry, that's shifting

1:30PM · Oct 23, 2019 · Twitter for iPhone

237

## The Great Resignation

 **Kim Crayton ~ Antiracist Economist ~ She/Her** 🌐
@KimCrayton1

It's easy, and let's be honest...lazy, to frame the "Great Resignation" as anything other than workers leveraging their ONLY real collective bargaining chip, labor, to demand that business leaders renegotiate the employer/employee relationship

Let's talk #ProfitWithOutOppression

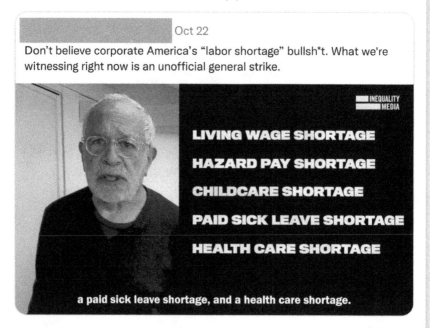

Oct 22

Don't believe corporate America's "labor shortage" bullsh*t. What we're witnessing right now is an unofficial general strike.

INEQUALITY MEDIA

LIVING WAGE SHORTAGE

HAZARD PAY SHORTAGE

CHILDCARE SHORTAGE

PAID SICK LEAVE SHORTAGE

HEALTH CARE SHORTAGE

a paid sick leave shortage, and a health care shortage.

7:25AM · Oct 23, 2021 · Twitter for iPhone

## White Women Are Not Diversity

White women are not diversity. White women do not come in with the unique, default perspective of "all women." They can only speak to the experiences they have as white women. Other than white men, white women are the greatest upholders of white supremacy, they literally give birth to and nurture future generations of racists, and historically abandon all solidarity efforts when asked to extend their support beyond "fighting against white men." White women will "fight the patriarchy" until they need the patriarchy to support them against being held accountable for their white supremacy. This is when they fall back into white tears, looking innocent and needing protection. This is when white men ride in to save them from the "angry Black women." White women's tears have contributed equally to the terror inflicted on members of racialized communities as white men's guns and ropes.

## Whiteness in Marginalized Spaces

When whiteness demands to be centered in marginalized spaces it causes harm. Whiteness is designed to center itself and will continue to do so unless checked. White folx need to actively demonstrate consistent, anti-racist behavior.

- Whiteness In Marginalized Spaces When Coalition Building Harms https://www.youtube.com/watch?v=ijpARXXrgpo
- Whiteness In Marginalized Spaces https://www.youtube.com/watch?v=UelQgl0YAVo

## The "Soft Skills" Myth

There are many folx in professional settings who only value a set of skills that can be easily codified e.g engineering, software development, data science, etc. While acquiring the skills to accomplish the basic job functions may be easier because they can be documented in a textbook [explicit knowledge], the more challenging aspects of those roles is developing the decision- making or logic capacities needed to inform those decisions [tacit knowledge], particularly if welcoming and psychological safety is a goal. It's these "soft skills," which is a term that I don't use–I prefer "human-centric skills"--that enable folx throughout the organization to leverage what they know in unique ways across domains. There's nothing "soft" about managing an organization's human assets. As the workforce moves closer to embracing diversity as an organizational asset, those folx who don't care to develop the skills needed for effective communication, for example, will find themselves struggling to remain relevant and  employable in a future of work that demands inclusion.

Also adopting a learning organization perspective necessitates that all internal stakeholders play a role in understanding the business and its desired goals and outcomes as a strategy for ensuring that efforts that drive innovation and differentiation are met. The days of software developers working in isolation with no collaborative effort being made to understand how the code base impacts the roles and responsibilities of others within the organization are over. Today's software developer is better informed on how to move forward with code-based decisions when they spend time understanding how other roles within the organization drive decisions related to products/services, PR/marketing, sales, HR, legal, content moderation, etc. Siloed thinking and decision-making continues to be direct threats to organizational level efforts of welcoming and psychological safety and mitigating harm.

## What is Organizational Hospitality?

- An organizational development strategy that is designed to aid in establishing an ethos of welcoming and psychological safety
- It's designed to help organizational leaders think critically about operationalizing their policies, procedures, and processes throughout the staffing life-cycle; from the invitation [recruiting] to the salutation/farewell [off-boarding].
- If PWO is the goal and welcoming and psychological safety is the "what," and having the ability to leverage organizational knowledge for innovation and gaining a competitive advantage is the "why," then Organizational Hospitality (OH) is the "how."
- Organizational leaders should see themselves as the hosts of an event:

  - Some hosts center themselves, leaving guests feeling unwelcomed and unsafe.
  - Other hosts center their guests, leaving guests feeling cared for, appreciated, welcomed, and safe
  - Helpful hint: Hosts who successfully center their guests have learned how to manage their feelings.
  - Leadership should see their role as being in service to labor because it aids in facilitating and nurturing an environment that can support the tenets of an effective learning organization.
  - Your level of responsibilities for establishing and maintaining organizational hospitality correlates to

the power and privilege an individual is able to leverage within an organization.

Organizational Hospitality Checklist: Provides a framework for measuring and managing welcoming and psychological safety across stakeholder domains. The score should be leveraged as data for those in leadership roles to base decisions. The checklist should be applied to measure and manage all stakeholders relationships. To do this, organizational leaders should think about the various touchpoints that would constitute the life-cycle for that relationship i.e., from the invitation to the salutation.

## How to score:

Organizational leaders need to evaluate and rate where they are related to each sub-domain:

- We have nothing (1);
- We have something (3);
- We have a policy, process, and/or procedure (5).

*Scoring each sub-domain should uniquely align with the core values and benchmarks that were developed in the "Know Thy Organization" section. In an effort to minimize my impact on biasing or influencing this process, I've decided not to include questions for you to answer and instead I've added to Appendix 2 the "PWO Event Planning Checklist" as a sample of the level of detail I engage in when doing this work with clients. Use it to dig deep, to go below the surface; align your policies, procedures, and processes with a supremacy-, coercion-, discrimination-, and exploitation-FREE perspective.*

Based on the score and these additional factors that aid in setting priorities, a strategy should be developed:

- What timeframe should be given to address:
  - immediate (within 30 days);
  - short-term (day 31 to 1 year);
  - and long-term (1 year+) .
- Plus a harm index:
  - high/active (definite);
  - medium/on the horizon (potential);
  - and low (none).

## Value of score:

- Helps develop the policies, procedures, and processes to measure and manage business outcomes
- Helps in prioritizing your effort and establishing time-frames/benchmarks
- Helps in communicating organizational strategy to stakeholders
- Helps to provide needed clarity for defining organizational roles and responsibilities
- Helps make the shift from traditional to PWO business model
- Helps make the shift from product/service focused to operationalizing core values focused

The OH Checklist for "those who work for you" is broken down into four  domains: Recruiting, Onboarding, Retaining, and Off-boarding [see sub-domains below].

## Recruiting

- Job Description
- Job Announcement
- Application Design
- Applicant Selection
- Interview Process
- Offer Negotiation
- Making An Offer

## Onboarding

- Feedback on the Onboarding Process
- Knowledge Organizational Sharing [Explicit/Tacit]
- Probation
- Peer Guide
- Orientation
- Joining [HR/Legal]

## Retaining

- Evaluation
- Promotion
- Mentoring
- Managing Your Feelings: I believe that unmanaged feelings in the workplace has an outsized unevaluated and detrimental influence on our ability to establish welcoming and psychological safety.
- Leadership and Management
- Giving and Receiving Feedback
- Training and Development

- Knowledge Transfer [Capture tacit knowledge before it walks out the door]
- Milestone Celebrations

## Offboarding

- References
- Termination
- Resignation
- Exit Interview
- Exiting HR/Legal i.e., the use of NDAs [non-disparagement agreement] to silence, particularly when tying folx's severance to signing, does not align with a supremacy-, coercion-, discrimination-, and exploitation-FREE workplace.

# Commentary

Adopting a PWO perspective for organizational development, a view that seeks supremacy-, coercion-, discrimination-, and exploitation-free, won't be easy but for many of us, the alternatives are just unacceptable. Prioritizing stakeholder vs. shareholder value will be challenged at every turn; trust me, ask my attorney. Our attempts at making even the simplest contracts less one-sided require creativity and the resources to fund such initiatives. Also, I recognize that it's a privilege even to have the resources to undertake such endeavors, as limited as they are. I also acknowledge that I'm not the first. Others have waded into these waters but where we differ is that I'm no longer attempting to mold the current "traditional" business model into what I desire. I'm no longer trying to parse out and cleave off the less harmful parts of systems, institutions, and policies designed to exclude, to accommodate my needs. I'm starting over. And I invite you to join me. There's a lot to do, and we get there together or not at all.

# Case Study: Paul

## What is your name and the nature of your business?

My name is Paul Campbell. I run a company called Tito and we build software for selling tickets on the Internet. During COVID, we built more software for running online events and building communities.

## How did you meet Kim?

The first time I met Kim was at Admission, a conference that my colleagues and I hosted in Chicago. It was a conference about running conferences and events. We were very mindful of producing an inclusive event. We also wanted the presentations to include expert perspectives on building inclusive and safe spaces. Kim had spoken at various tech conferences around the world—our software was mostly used by the tech conference market—so she came up on my colleague's radar and became the de facto keynote speaker of that event. She got up and said to the crowd, "*I need you to get comfortable with being uncomfortable.*" I had no idea what that meant. I also had no idea of how bad things could be for people who don't look like me and have the privilege that I have. I got thrown in the deep end. I didn't simply attend the presentation, I experienced it. It will stay with me forever. There was an anger, but it wasn't angry. It was raw and direct. I don't remember the slides or the specific academic content, but I do remember how it made me feel. That was Kim.

That was the first part, experiencing that presentation.

The second part was the look on Kim's face later in the day. We'd all gotten to know each other a bit better and the talks were done. We were into the more social part of the event and transformed the venue from a relaxed conference venue to an even more relaxed dining room. We had hired some chefs to come in and cook a meal for everyone. Kim delighted at that, just doing her thing and being part of this wild adventure in building relationships. It stood out in contrast to the visceral message from earlier in the day. For Kim, that meal was pure joy and comradery.

That was the day I met Kim. A fiery introduction followed by a warm experience of dining together, chatting, winding down for the day, reveling in life.

### Though you do not remember the slides in the presentation, you said you remember how it made you feel.

Before that presentation and subsequent interactions, I often found myself wanting to pursue inclusivity out of an abstract obligation. In some sense, our efforts were simply box-checking. I wasn't inhabiting the mind space of the individuals I wanted to include. I wanted to be seen as inclusive but I didn't have the experience, the vocabulary, or the insight to articulate why.

During her talk, I felt a lot of things. I don't want to say it was simply just guilt, anger, or shame but it was a feeling in the realm of those three. Kim set expectations that birthed discomfort in my own shoes, but she was trying to put across the message that what is uncomfortable for me is the default for many.

Later, working with Kim involved coaching and reading and listening to information that made me understand a marginalized person's perspective more. This led to a mindset shift. But that first day, I came away with a feeling that I was missing something. A feeling of I'm not doing enough. A feeling that maybe there *was* a lot to learn.

## How did being enlightened make you think differently?

The following time I met Kim was a few months later in London at a workshop for marginalized folks she was hosting. I remember saying something quite awkward. Without missing a step, she told me that what I'd said was inappropriate, but she didn't say it was wrong to say it. She let me say it and she addressed it. Though I said what I said out of curiosity, when I saw the response I was quite embarrassed. I remember her later saying *"I've got work to do with you. You really need work."*

I had no idea what she meant but my initial response to everything she was saying was a combination of arrogance and defensiveness. I ended up looking for false equivalences to demonstrate my position. One of those is the identity of being Irish. I've seen this in my parents, and certain individuals in the past who bring up how Irish people at one point in history were oppressed.

Irish people endured a lot, but throughout history they were never bought or sold as property. It takes work but it can be true to say that treatment of Irish folks was deplorable but that it never came close to the establishment of chattel slavery from Africa to America. The experiences that Irish people suffered through is one category of misfortune, but it is an entirely different category to being reduced to possessions that can be bought and sold. It's a different category. That was something Kim had to instill in me. It was uncomfortable to acknowledge but through discomfort, I was able to get a tiny sense of what living with this is like.

Next was learning about how Irish people became "white." Irish folks were able to integrate and conform in a way that people of color, particularly in the United States, could not.

Thirdly was understanding that this problem is not limited to the United States. I have friends who say *"I don't want to learn about the history of slavery in the United States because it's got nothing to do with me in Scotland or England or Ireland or Australia."* You do not need to go very far into history to see that this is a global problem. As Kim often repeats, anti-Blackness is a worldwide phenomenon. Black women are likely to be treated the worst wherever in the world they are.

Before learning and reading on the recommendation of Kim, I was in a bit of denial about things in Ireland. To my shame, *"Oh, racism doesn't really exist in Ireland so much"* is a real thought I had.

If you follow Black people online who live in Ireland, as I did, the idea that racism isn't a problem in Ireland is simply absurd. It's unfortunately a worldwide problem. Kim did not explicitly show me this, and even if she had I probably wouldn't have listened. She did, however, give me the tools and appetite to go looking to find that it is a local problem to me in addition to being a problem in the United States. My perspective was only informed by my limited bubble. As Kim says, knowledge is power. Knowledge is the first step in recognizing there is a problem, so she has helped me to recognize problems where otherwise I wouldn't even have thought to look.

## When you said she gave you the tools, what kind of tools did she empower you with?

Kim has her guiding principles. We don't follow them explicitly in the company, but they're useful as a lens with which to view things differently than the typical white-male-dominated power structure perspective that we inherited by osmosis simply growing up reasonably comfortably in Ireland and going to private school in Ireland. Ireland is still majority white and under the influence of the Catholic church. There has been increasing diversity throughout my life here but in terms of politics it's mostly white and mostly male, just like in the UK, Europe, and the rest of the Western world.

Kim regularly intentionally overshares examples of her guiding principles either being reinforced or being broken. So, the guiding principle that there's no such thing as apolitical tech is a huge statement in itself. For example, when I got into coding, there was no question whether it was political. I even studied politics, and tech and politics just seemed like two completely opposite ends of the spectrum. However, if you look back through history, technology and politics have been intertwined since forever. Technology is what drove people forward, generated wealth, and won wars, but it's so easy to ignore how they are interdependent. Kim's perspective gave me a new understanding of that relationship.

Another principle—inclusion being risk management—just makes sense. It's straight up science. If you act in an exclusive way, you're including the folks who are within one circle. However, if you act by prioritizing the most vulnerable, you're not excluding people you've included prior. You're just including more people and the idea that *that* could be a problem now makes no sense to me whatsoever. Acting inclusively by default simply makes logical sense.

This leads to one of those other revelations that I had working with Kim. I would often see a world event or a company do something silly or say something that would get people's noses out of shape. It wouldn't make sense to me why they acted this way or the other. This is because I was trying to make sense of things from the wrong perspective. Somebody was trying to make some money here or somebody was trying to push this or that person out and it wasn't logical. It was probably likely to be an emotional decision from somewhere.

Early when working with Kim, she would challenge me on something and I would get upset. Thankfully I don't remember the specific examples now but invariably, I would sleep on it and if I looked at things from an emotional perspective, we would end up with my conclusion. However, if we took the logical, objective outcome, we'd end up with Kim's. Sometimes that was what she had to do. She had to really beat into us these conclusions that followed the logic, but we couldn't see the logic because we were letting our emotions dictate our outcomes. This is quite a common theme amongst privileged individuals who have decision-making power.

Being able to spot patterns is critical, and Kim speaks about these patterns that whiteness always paints itself as the hero or the victim and never the villain. Knowledge is power. If you can actually see yourself as a villain in certain circumstances, then you can adjust and move on and maybe solve the problem without feeling like you're under attack or putting yourself on a pedestal. It's powerful and obviously nobody wants to be the villain, but sometimes knowing that you're the villain leads to a better outcome or more inclusive outcome, and that's a powerful notion.

**If you had to say the most impactful message and/or sentiment that Kim has alerted you to that has caused you to conduct business differently, what would that single message be?**

Amongst my peer group, some of whom are very successful financially, there has been a theme of attempting to reinvent from first principles. That always made logical sense to me. If we question how a system is built, then it would make sense to go back to first principles and attempt to make the system better. It just always felt like an approach that was self-evidently virtuous to a certain degree. The coaching that we've been through has led me to question the implicit assumption that going back to the first principles always leads to a "better" result. Kim would say *"Who is it better for?"* Without that follow-up question, we're in the realm of platitudes. That is so obvious in hindsight, but I don't think I would have gotten there by myself.

Kim has no problem with rethinking from first principles, but the addition would be to question why the established systems exist in the first place. For example, an unwieldy HR process that requires a lot of paperwork might slow the process of HR down from one perspective but from another perspective, it might represent a rigorous adherence to a process that applies fairness across the board. What do we gain by rethinking things? What do we lose?

The biggest lesson that Kim has left us with as a team is to always question our first assumptions about any decision. It's not about being more right or wrong, it's about applying a broader perspective. We now recognize there are important perspectives outside of our own that we may not understand. We may not be able to articulate them at first, but discovering them may lead to a different decision than we might have taken otherwise. We should go looking for different perspectives before moving forward.

## What do you say to Kim to keep her encouraged in this work now that you have recognized it can be arduous and a lot for one person?

I try to follow the advice of people I trust who I deem to be smarter or more clued-in than I am. Invariably, people who I trust a lot, I boost, and I think Kim deserves to be boosted. I think that she brings such a combination of energy, enthusiasm, humanity, and knowledge that it is impossible not to learn from her and not to feel responsible for carrying her message that she brings on behalf of many thousands, if not hundreds of thousands or millions of individuals. Her work is worthwhile, and her work is working. More people need to be part of the work, and that will happen as her profile grows as it has and it should.

## Is there anything else that you'd like to add that we have not discussed?

I think the process of working with my colleagues is in a far better place than it was ahead of working with Kim. It became a more tangible outcome as we went through a challenging coaching process. We have been through a process that led to identifying core values, making values-driven decisions, and evaluating our own behavior objectively. Kim completely changed the interpersonal dynamic of our company, leading to clearer communication, lower stress, and stronger working relationships. For me, that's huge.

# Case Study: Doc

## When you first met Kim, what was the nature of the working relationship?

Kim was booked in as a speaker for a gathering of event organizers that we ran back in 2018. Before I met Kim in person, a funny anecdote, we had started to invite people to the conference, and were giving out a few free tickets to various conference people in Chicago where the event was being held. During this process, I ended up getting into an interaction via DM on Twitter with someone we offered a ticket to. He was clearly trying to push his own agenda saying we didn't have a diverse lineup. This was coming from a middle-aged white guy. He seemed to take offense that our lineup was made up mainly of women, and he was complaining that not enough men were being represented, so that was already a red flag to start. We decided to rescind the invitation for him to join us, and his response was to publicly @mention all of the speakers on Twitter, saying *"If you go and speak at this conference, you will be harming your reputation."* Not a particularly good start to our first conference. I tried to get ahead of this and emailed all the speakers, saying *"Listen, this had just happened, this is why it happened, here is a transcription of the conversations I have had with this guy. My advice would be to ignore him, and with a bit of luck, he will disappear back into the ether."* I left my phone number and said if anyone wants to get in touch, feel free. About 30 seconds after I sent that email, Kim rang me, which was my first interaction with her. She asked who this guy was and what did he think he was doing talking about her reputation on Twitter. She thanked me for the email but said she could not ignore him and she would have to deal with it, and I said okay. I quipped that people like him are why Twitter was so toxic and her response was something like *"Twitter may be toxic but for people like me, it gives us a voice we never would have had."* She immediately gave me a perspective I'd never thought about. She then went on to teach the guy a valuable lesson on why talking about someone's reputation in public isn't a good idea. So that was my first interaction with Kim, and obviously not under the best circumstances, but it showed me who Kim was and what she was about. She wasn't about to have some random guy talk trash about her on Twitter for no reason.

We subsequently met in person in Chicago at that conference in 2018, and we got along extremely well. She spoke about things I hadn't thought about from her perspective as a Black woman in the tech scene from Atlanta, Georgia. It kind of blew my mind with the experiences she had, of course some good, some bad. It was just a whole new perspective on an area that I thought I knew but of course only, as a white guy going to conferences in Europe. So very much a learning experience from day one. Kim closed out the conference and it went really well, but I wanted to get her advice on something before everyone left. We had recently grown the company from four to 10 people, we were an all-white team, and we knew that was a problem. There were excuses for why this happened but none of them was anything that my co-founder Paul or I was happy with, and it had been something weighing heavily on my mind. We wanted to find a solution for how to go forward, and I had been looking for someone to help us because we didn't have the internal experience to correctly and properly diversify the team. Thankfully, she agreed to help us and that is where the relationship as our business coach started a few months after that.

Crucially, Kim's approach to us solving our diversity problem wasn't to go out and help find more diverse candidates. It was to get the company to a place where it was a safe place to work for anyone working there. She explained this would take time and there was no quick fix.

Kim had worked with other companies before and had a framework to help us, but the main thing she was pushing us to do was embrace a number of pillars she had developed for trying to get businesses to look internally. The first thing was defining our core values, which we didn't have. We had sort of an underlying idea of what the company was about, but we had never sat down and written anything on paper. Kim had a number of exercises to get us to the point where we could accurately describe our core values, and that was the first step. I know it might seem small, but it actually had a big impact on us as a business and on us as colleagues as well. Once we had a set of core values, that gave us a framework internally to start judging things and using them to make decisions if ever there was a disagreement. In the past, we would often get into arguments or the management would get in a deadlock on which way to proceed. Once we had those core values in place, it was a lot easier to move forward on these types of things. So they had a huge effect on the company, like I said, for the interaction between management and passing those core values to the rest of the team.

## What is your company, when did it start, and who do you serve?

We are Team Tito. It's a small company that started off building software, and our first platform is Tito. It's a platform for organizers to sell tickets to their events and conferences. We started as three or four people and since then, we have grown and shrunk a little bit due to COVID impacting the events' industry. So we went up to 10, we are now back down to six, but yes, our main platform is Tito. At the beginning of COVID, we started working on a second platform called Vito, which is an online community and events platform where customers can create hubs for running events either in person or online. We're a fully remote team based out of Ireland with an office in the city center of Dublin, but most people work from home or elsewhere. We have three team members who work abroad in England and Scotland.

## What was your reason for starting this company?

My co-founder Paul was someone who used to run a lot of events, and he didn't like the existing solutions that were available at the time. A lot of them were overpriced, slow, and difficult to use. He wanted the experience of attending an event to start with the website and the ticket purchasing flow rather than when they turn up at the venue. So we wanted to be able to provide folks with a more delightful way of purchasing tickets for an event. Delight is one of our core values, but it is generally not associated with purchasing tickets online. The archaic systems in place at the time were very difficult to use. It was costly and not very forgiving from the user interface point of view. So we wanted something easy to use, a much nicer experience, so that is why we started that particular platform. Similarly, with Vito, many of the online systems out there for events were quite clunky. Obviously, quite a few systems have sprung up over the last couple of years due to COVID, but we wanted Vito to be a better, safer experience for people—a more delightful experience.

## Describe the people you serve.

Our customers tend to be people who run their own events, similarly to Paul, a lot of community tech events. Funny enough, we don't have a huge number of customers in our native Ireland but most are in the U.S., Europe, Australia, and Canada. I think people use Tito for a few different reasons, obviously the simple interface and the more user-friendly approach to purchasing tickets, but I also think because we have been around for quite a long time now. I think the first version of Tito was in 2013. What we try to do is make sure we look out for our customers as best as we can. I think since we are a small team, a lot of people know they are going to get a nicer level of service from us, as opposed to other bigger companies where they are just another customer. We tend to be more aware of who our customers are, what they are doing, and try to help them as much as we can. We have always been quite responsive to customer support and have a good reputation based on that. It's one of those industries where folks can get quite easily panicked when they are selling tickets to their events or putting tickets on sale. Because we have run our own events, we are familiar with it and we can put ourselves in their shoes.

## What does a professional like Kim and her messaging, strategies, and level of awareness call us to? How is that beneficial to a business like yours?

The core values were a great start and really changed how we worked day-to-day, but speaking to Kim on a weekly basis—and it has been for a couple of years now—we have been able to change how we run our company by making sure we lay the groundwork for the future, prioritizing the most vulnerable for example.

The key to doing this was that we needed to spend more time working "on" the business instead of "in" the business, something we were definitely guilty of. Again it seems obvious, but I believe this is quite common for a lot of founder-led tech companies. None of us went to management school, we hadn't had education on how to run a business, and Kim has helped us with that. Obviously we want the business to be growing and to be the best place it can be for the people working on the team, but we used to struggle with what to do to achieve that. Even just teaching us how to resolve conflicts within the team. If there was something that has caused an issue, we'd discuss it at the next coaching session. Kim wouldn't necessarily solve things for us, but gave us the tools over time to be able to resolve these things ourselves.

Going back to the original reason we started talking with Kim about diversifying our team, she has helped us to produce inclusive job descriptions, put together an inclusive company handbook, and make our work environment a place where we prioritize the most vulnerable. With the job descriptions, for example, I would write the first draft, and Kim would then highlight all the things that could be seen as red flags to someone who wasn't a white guy. They weren't deliberate, but I had underlying biases based on my single lived experience. Kim was able to identify these things and show them to us while explaining to us why someone who doesn't look like us would walk away from that job based on what was written. So that has been hugely helpful to us.

I think she also helped us to really focus on the important things in running the business. It's very easy if you are an engineer by trade or designer by trade and you're now running a company to fall back into working on the product because it's familiar and comfortable and maybe shy away from some of the bigger-picture things. Take the company handbook for example. This is something Kim and I have been working on for the last few months and up until this point, we just had a standard cookie cutter template provided by our HR company. It's one of those things that people would wave their hands up saying *"Oh it's fine, we don't need to spend time on that, we are a small team."* But that isn't right. Even within a small team, we need to make sure everyone is comfortable and their experience in the company is the best it can be. Having a properly put-together employee handbook where everything is covered, including the policies and procedures, lets people know where they stand, and that is something we had been missing. Having weekly conversations with Kim helps us to focus on those parts of the business that would be ignored otherwise. So from the top down, Kim has helped the business and helped us know where to focus our time as the leadership team.

## Have you seen the impact Kim has had on your business?

Absolutely since day one, since we first had our initial conversation and were able to start defining and adopting our core values. That impacted everything from big decisions to little code or user interface changes. It gives us a set of standards written down to refer to and it means, more importantly, everyone is on the same page. We have obviously shared the core values throughout the team. We have defined them, and everyone is aware of them. There is no ambiguity or question when someone is working on something if this adheres to core values or not. Having these written down and having them repeated frequently during team meetings helps to drive it down to the rest of the team and have everybody sit with it in the back of their minds when they are working day-to-day. It goes down into the details as well.

## What would you say to the business that just goes forward without the level of intentionality that Kim calls to the forefront? What would you say to the business owner?

I would probably say they are doomed for failure at some point, particularly when people are now talking about a tech recession and a lot of businesses are slowing hiring or laying off staff. It's the Silicon Valley approach of chasing growth at all costs because of pressure from their investors. The *"move fast and break things"* attitude which is so harmful. So many tech companies aren't built as safe, sustainable businesses, and are starting to suffer because of that. Uber is one of the examples where they are losing however many millions every month because the company was created to be all about growth at any cost. I think that is incredibly dangerous. While we are still small is the time to put in the effort. We said we weren't going to grow the business and we weren't going to hire any more people until we had a proper employee handbook, correct job descriptions, things like that because the bigger you get, the harder it is to backwards engineer it. I think having the lessons that Kim teaches us is crucial and we would have benefited greatly from having her insight at an earlier stage. It would have saved us a lot of internal strife. Concentrating on the business rather than the product at an earlier stage certainly would have helped us. So yeah, the earlier you can look at these fundamentals, the better. Creating a business is hard and working with Kim has helped us create a more inclusive and safer team environment. Ultimately, that is the goal. An inclusive company is going to be a more successful one at the end of the day.

## Final thoughts to Kim

Kim has changed how we work, how I see things, and how the team interacts, particularly with myself and my co-founder Paul. I wish we'd had her sooner, but there is no time like the present. She has helped us in many ways. A big thank you to Kim.

# Profit Without Oppression

*Not asking permission...giving notice!*

*—Kim Crayton—*

The systems, institutions, and policies in place teach Black women that success is in our academic accomplishments. The higher we go in academia, the greater we are. I am now in a place where I am rejecting this. I am no longer in a place where I feel I need to prove my worth and value to people, places, and things that inherently see me as valueless. Working on my doctorate degree became so taxing, I was anxious to simply log into my account. It was a years-long battle in my head of *"There is work to do. Why aren't you doing the work? Are you lazy?"* I was filled with these internalized thoughts that I wasn't doing enough but in reality, I just did not want to do it. I recognized that I had been living with low-grade anxiety. The work I do is a challenge and so much of what we experience is behind the scenes, whispered emotions. We don't know about it and as a result we internalize it and make it our fault. When it came to my doctorate, I was on this schedule and I had to meet these benchmarks, but that isn't how my brain works. I take information in, I process,

I play, and then I ask myself, *"Do I understand it or not?"* I am not a person who can just read something and write it, even if it is a topic I already know. I wasn't getting that from the process with my doctoral program. I was getting that from my work. I loved the research that I was doing, but the process of logging in and seeing messages from my committee members was not motivating me to the finish line. I didn't care about their grades. I cared about the work that I was doing. The thought of working on something when the work wasn't fully formed was anxiety-inducing. Understanding this and accepting it allowed me to call academia what it was: Another system that was not built for me.

Academia is no different than any other system, institution or policy. It is rooted in white supremacy and anti-Blackness and is not designed to accommodate us. In fact, many of its institutions were built on the backs of slaves and from the profits of the global slave trade. The only people happy in academia are cis, hetero, Christian white dudes. Academia is not playful, joyful, peaceful, or liberating for most. All others are experiencing some form of hell. For Black people, the last thing we were supposed to do was get a K-12 education, let alone a doctorate degree. Embracing our Blackness; its impact and influence on our scholarship isn't a thing, particularly if doing so means challenging the false narrative of the "greatness of whiteness". We are only tolerated in these spaces when we assimilate and whitewash our lived experiences and our work for the comfort of the same cis, hetero, Christian white dudes. Our acceptance, in these spaces, is contingent on our willingness to prioritize whiteness; including adopting the mannerisms and aesthetics of white folx.

For example, I always took feedback from my committee personally because it "felt personal." Although we followed a rubric, their comments always seemed subjective and inconsistent, it was challenging at times just processing it. It took me hiring a Black woman, who coaches people through the doctoral process, to help me understand why the experience was so triggering. She said, *"Kim, you have to realize that they see their job as to 'tear your work apart' in order to make it better."* Now, I don't have a problem with being critiqued or receiving feedback, but if your idea of improving my work stems solely from negative reinforcement of simply tearing folx apart then I want no part of that because its rooted in supremacy, coercion, discrimination, and exploitation. As an educator and business strategist, I work hard to provide clear and objective feedback to students and clients. Most of the feedback I received from my committee was often unclear. One person would say it was okay, the other would say it wasn't. It left me lost. Yet, I was being held accountable for things I did not understand. I needed support. I needed help to process what I was experiencing, and Black women became that support; my lifeline.

It was Black women, in academia, who let me know that what I was experiencing was not unique and that I wasn't alone. Before I found this community of Black women scholars, I didn't understand nor could I articulate what I was experiencing so, I tried to do what many of them did, simply tell myself to put my head down and push through but at the same time, I couldn't stop asking myself "why are you doing this; is the degree worth all the trauma?" Especially when what I was experiencing was in complete contrast to everything I was pouring into this book. By the time I was wrapping up the "Know Thy Community" section of the book, I had decided that it was time to walk away because finishing my doctoral program did not align with what I am building. I have no strong desire to have my work in peer-reviewed articles, in fact that does not align with what I am building. I was reminded that the systems, institutions, and policies of exclusion that are "higher ed" were the reason I was writing this book. It is to get this information into the hands of as many folx as possible. To take the knowledge I gained from these cloistered spaces to the masses. I also began to understand that these folx are not my peers.

In academia, white dudes have had their paths cleared, manicured, and polished, while my path, and that of other Black women, is covered with rocks and glass. My getting to the end cannot be compared to their getting to the end because I've had to put in more work. I no longer see them as my competition. They are also not my target audience. Much of academia is about debate and critique, but I do not trust the opinions of most of these people and I do not want them critiquing and debating my work. They do not come from a nuanced perspective or lived experience. As far as I am concerned, they are not qualified to debate or critique my scholarship. That is how Black women saved me because they told me they all go through this. They let me in on these horror stories of how their health was affected, and I made a decision to no longer jump through hoops for people and places that do not value me and will not value my work.

Breaking out of that "fear" of being perceived as lazy or a quitter has brought me so much peace. My coach said to me one day, *"Kim, you are overwhelmed, you are not underproducing."* What she said hit me. When we are not moving per the systems, institutions, and policies that were designed to privilege the few at the expense of the many we internalize it, and that is what I was doing. Not anymore. I do not have the low-grade anxiety that I wasn't even aware of until I stopped pursuing this "dream" of being a Dr. I also realized that gaining a title of "Dr." would create a barrier between me and the audiences I want to reach. That it would make me and the work less approachable for some whom I wish to reach. There is an expectation for people with doctorates that I do not want to be a part of. I want my scholarship to reach the masses. I want my scholarship to reach those who should not have to go to school and into this much financial debt to learn this information. I will share and publish my work the way I want to. Stepping away from my doctoral program means I am stepping away from the supremacy, coercion, discrimination, and exploitation that it was founded on. I realized that I needed the ability to move around the world with an intrinsic knowing that I am of value outside of systems, institutions, and policies designed to make me question this as often as I breathe.

Black women do not get the benefit of the doubt. When we enter these spaces we don't get to say *"Slow down. I do not understand."* We must figure it out or we get fired or punished. Trying to fit myself into this was too much. I love research. I learned what I needed to learn, and I now know that I should have left then. I should not have tried to force myself to finish when that was not my purpose for starting. I started school to learn about business and I was not getting it anywhere else, so I went where the already powerful and privileged went to get this type of information. Once I got the information, I started sharing it with my clients. I was also already receiving feedback from clients that let me know that I was achieving my goal of democratizing business school education. That I didn't have to wait to raise my prices when "I got my degree"; what was I waiting on? I was conflating more into the doctorate than I even believed.

To Black women who are at a point of walking away, I want you to know it is time. Validation and acceptance from these systems, institutions, and policies is not about acceptance for you. It is about assimilation and not accommodating you. This is why they have to make laws such as The Crown Act. The Crown Act should not be a thing. I should be able to go to work any way I want to. I am here to give you permission that if anything, whether professional or personal, is not aligning to where you want to be, walk away. Know Thy Self. Seeing value in yourself, valuing your mental health, is more important than anything. We can never be our authentic self if we continue to put ourselves in molds of other people. I do not need anyone to validate me; nor do you. Black women, who are the moral compass, need the freedom to do the work that society needs to heal; we need to be liberated and our collective freedom is through us. My hope is that  this book will assist you with that. My hope is that you will embrace my mantra: "Not Asking Permission...Giving Notice!"

# CTA: Get To Work

*"It's time for those with the power and privilege to make change to get off their asses and take action."*

*—Kim Crayton—*

Now that you have read this book, I want you to get off your ass and get to work. Y'all asked for a strategy for moving forward. For building the world and future that we want to see. So here it is; now it's time for y'all to get to damn work. To abandon all of your excuses for why you're not contributing. As an educator, I believe that you can't hold people accountable for things they don't understand. This book isn't written to be your one-stop shop for developing your consistent, DEMONSTRATED antiracist practice, but it's a good start. Building a future that is supremacy-, coercion-, discrimination-, and exploitation-free won't be easy but it will be worth our effort. So you must see this work. This book is a must-have. Let's try to create a world that was never supposed to exist. And I'll leave you with this question: "What kind of ancestor do you want to be?"

Recognize that systems, institutions, and policies are designed to privilege the few by excluding the many. If you desire to shift the system, here is what you can do next. Develop your consistent, demonstrated antiracist practice by taking the following actions:

- **LISTEN**: Antiracist Economy podcast with Kim Crayton
- **ACTIVATE**: (1) Host an event. (2) Become a "The Future Is FREE" volunteer.
- **FELLOWSHIP:** Join the Profit Without Oppression Community Hub.
- **SPONSOR:** Fund the independent research.

All these actions and more can be accessed via the following link:
https://linktr.ee/TheFutureIsFREE

# Profitable Playlist

**HERE ARE 14 OF MY FAVORITE SONGS TO KEEP YOU INSPIRED, MOTIVATED, AND UPLIFTED.**

1. Swagga Like Us — T.I, Jay-Z
2. 24K Magic — Bruno Mars
3. Welcome to Atlanta — Jermaine Dupri, Ludacris
4. Lose Yourself — Eminem
5. All Eyez On Me — 2Pac
6. I'm Every Woman — Witney Houston
7. Yeah! — Usher, Lil Jon, Ludacris
8. It's Raining Men — The Weather Girls
9. Pon de Replay — Rihanna
10. The Boss — Diana Ross
11. Higher — Dj Khaled, Nipsey Hussle, John Legend
12. Double Dutch Bus — Frankie Smith
13. Don't Cha — The Pussycat Dolls, Busta Rhymes
14. Whole Lotta Woman — Kelly Clarkson

# Appendix 1:
# The Powell Memo

The Powell Memo (1971) was commissioned by the U.S. Chamber of Commerce http://law2.wlu.edu/deptimages/ Powell%20Archives/PowellMemorandumTypescript.pdf

I use this version of the Powell Memo because it's a copy of the orginal and not someone else's interpretation or understanding.

# Appendix 2: Profit Without Oppression Event Planning Checklist

## Client Details:

- Event's Name
- Event's Location(s)
- Event's Dates
- Event's Target Audience
- Event's Expected Attendance
- Event's Organizational Leaders
- Organizational Leaders Demographic Makeup

## Before

## LOGISTICS:

- Is this a new event? If not, how many times has it been produced?

- What data have you collected from previous events?
- When is the event?
- Where will the event be held?
- How many members are on your organizing team?
- Do any of those members identify as underrepresented or marginalized?
- If so, how many?
- Are any of those members financially compensated?
- If not, why?
- What decision-making roles do these individuals hold within the organizing team?
- Are their perspectives included in decisions related to content, partnerships, financial, etc.?
- Are any of the vendor businesses that are providing services for your event owned by individuals who identify as members of underrepresented or marginalized groups?
- Does your marketing include gender-neutral language and images?
- Is your website accessible?
- Are you utilizing a boilerplate CoC?

## ATTENDEES:

- Have you budgeted for attendance scholarships for underrepresented and marginalized individuals?
- Are you collecting demographic information at the time of registration?
- Are attendees offered an opportunity to contribute to a scholarship fund?

## SPEAKERS:

- Are you compensating all speakers? If not, why?

- Are you compensating any speakers? If so, what metrics are you using to determine who gets compensated?
- Do any of your compensated speakers identify as members of underrepresented or marginalized groups in tech?
- If not, what metrics did you use to determine not to compensate members of underrepresented or marginalized groups in tech for their expertise?
- Are all speakers' expenses being covered, including travel, accommodations, food, and incidentals?
- If not, are you covering any speaker expenses? Which ones?
- What factors lead to deciding only these expenses?
- How are your speakers chosen: blind, invited, a mix, or other?
- Based on your speaker selection process, what is your demographic breakdown?
- Do you have a demographic goal?
- Did you meet that goal?
- How often are members of your organizing team attending events that are attended by underrepresented and marginalized individuals to build relationships?
- Have you created a speaker guidebook that details all speaker related information, i.e travel, accommodations, travel to venue, hotel information, talk details and requirements, etc.?
- Are speaker's travel and accommodations booked by the organizing team?
- If not, are speakers expected to pay for their travel and accommodations and be reimbursed?
- What's the turnaround time for reimbursements?
- How are travel and accommodations covered if speaker informs you that they are unable to prepay and wait for reimbursement?

## SPONSORS/VENDOR:

- Do your sponsors/vendors have an established reputation of inclusion within their organizations?
- Are sponsors contributing to scholarship fund?

## VENUE:

- Will the event and accommodations be held at the same venue? If not, what is the plan for speakers who need downtime?
- Have you negotiated low or no-cost incidentals for speakers (place a block on their room unless they use their cards)?
- If not, have you included that fee information in your speaker guidebook?
- Is the venue located near other venues or attractions that may cause attendees to violate the event's CoC, i.e., strip clubs, massage parlors, bars, etc.?
- Have you provided specific directions to the venue?
- If you are recommending attendees use public transportation, have you personally traveled the route, documenting landmarks and signage?
- Getting to the venue:

## PUBLIC TRANSPORT

- Is there a public transportation stop near the venue?
- Are public transportation stops accessible to people using mobility devices?
- Are public transportation stops accessible to people using service animals?

- Are public transportation stops accessible to people who are sight impaired?
- Is the area around the venue safe and well-lit?

## PARKING

- How close is parking to the venue?
- Are there costs associated with parking?
- Is the parking lot well-lit?
- Is the parking lot gated?
- Is the parking lot guarded?

## ACCESSING THE VENUE

- Is there any building security?
- What is the process for entering?
- Are there steps going into the building or space?
- Are there ramps or elevators?
- Are elevator buttons of an appropriate height for wheelchair users to reach?
- Is there affordable childcare at or near the venue?

## THE VENUE

- Is there a quiet room?
- Is there a nursing room for mothers with a newborn?
- Is the venue safe for small children?
- Is the space easily navigable for people using mobility devices or service animals?
- Do chairs in the venue have arms?
- Are food and (non-alcoholic) drinks allowed in the space?

- How many bathrooms (both single and multiple occupancy) are available?
- How many handicap stalls or single-occupancy bathrooms are there?
- How many gender-neutral bathrooms are available? If none, is it possible to make some gender neutral?

## During

### LOGISTICS:

- How will you communicate with attendees and speakers?
- Is the organizing/leadership team easy to identify if needed?
- Do you have a CoC?
- Is it a boilerplate? Customized?
- Has your team been trained on communicating and, when necessary, enforcing the CoC?
- Have you created a creative, engaging method for sharing the CoC beyond text, i.e. airline's flight safety steps?

### ATTENDEES:

- Will any meals be provided?
- What dietary restrictions are you prepared to accommodate?
- Have the leadership team planned on hosting any events that do not include alcohol?

### SPEAKERS:

- Will speakers be using their own equipment?

- Is there time scheduled to test speaker equipment?
- Will there be a speaker's dinner?
- Is there a member of the team assigned to greet speakers and handle any issues they may have, i.e. check-in, registration, presentation logistics, local travel, etc.?

## SPONSORS/VENDOR:

- Do sponsors understand and have they agreed to abide by the CoC?
- Do sponsors understand how to report any potential CoC violations?
- Have sponsors considered or intend to host any non-alcoholic events?
- Are sponsors using gender-neutral language in their marketing materials?

## VENUE:

- Is someone assigned to handle any venue/hotel issues?

# After (30 Days Later)

## LOGISTICS:

- Have you paid all expenses within the agreed upon timeframe?
- If the event made a profit, were any of the funds shared with any unpaid support volunteers or speakers?
- Have you addressed all CoC issues that may have come up during the event?
- Did you meet your demographic goals?

- If so, what have you learned and will that knowledge be used for future events? How?
- If not, what have you learned and will that knowledge be used for future events? How?

## ATTENDEES:

- Have you sent attendees a "thank you"?
- Have you sent attendees a follow-up feedback survey?

## SPEAKERS:

- Have you provided speakers with feedback?
- Have you paid all agreed upon speaker expenses?
- Have you sent speakers a "thank you"?
- Have you sent speakers a follow-up feedback survey?

## SPONSORS/VENDORS:

- Have you sent sponsors/vendors a "thank you"?
- Have you sent sponsors/vendors a follow-up feedback survey?

## VENUE:

- Have all questions/comments/concerns, if any, been raised and resolved with the venu

# Appendix 3: Words You Must Stop Using to Describe Marginalized Folx in the Workplace:

| STOP USING | | INSTEAD USE |
|:---:|:---:|:---:|
| aggressive | → | assertive |
| intimidating | → | sure/confident |
| defensive | → | committed |
| emotional | → | passionate |
| angry | → | determined |
| overreactive | → | justified |

# Appendix 4: Dismantling White Supremacy And The 5 Stages of Grief

*I've chosen to add this article, which was originally published as a Medium post November 6, 2018 because, as I wrap up writing this book in November 2022, nothing much has changed. White folx are still struggling to effectively address their role in maintaining white supremacy.*

So, for many white people, the past two years have been sort of a earth-shattering wakeup call regarding the realities of living in the United States and in many other parts of the world.

Many of you found your comfort in believing the fairytale that you were living in a "post racial" world and that, some how, we'd all found a way to get along. You were happy. Many of you even challenged members of marginalized communities when we made any attempts to talk about our lived experiences in a country that used racial ideology to justify the enslavement and the extermination of people for economic gain.

For the few white people who were even aware of the true racial reality that existed and that you worked hard to counter, you thought your work was done. You assumed that everyone was finally on the same page. But that all changed on November 6, 2016 because that was the day that, through the efforts of redrawing district boundaries, voter suppression, and a history of racists policies, WHITE PEOPLE elected a person for president who embodies everything about the white supremacist's nature of this country.

So here we are again.

It is November 6, 2018, a full two years later and some of you, and your lives are falling apart. You are now not only aware of racism's hold on your lives and your history but also, you are grappling with the fact that you just may not be as "great" and "talented" as you've been taught that you are. For the first time, for most, you are questioning everything you have been told about yourself and the "others" around you.

You've lost friends you cared about. There are members of your family who you no longer speak to. There are jokes, stories, and conversations being told in your places of work that you no longer laugh at or participate in. Some of you on this day, can admit that you have lost your TRUE NORTH and you are in a lot of pain.

What you are feeling is only a portion of the pain, agony, terror, and oppression that millions of members of marginalized communities experience every day of our lives. The stress of the internal, ongoing monologue that plays, like a loop, in our minds when we enter spaces or have experiences that require us to evaluate our safety and well-being. Checking our TONE, body language, and even our physical proximity to whiteness in order to gauge who we have to be, what we need to say, and how we need to say it in order to maintain the maximum comfort for you.

Oh, by the way...IT IS FUCKING EXHAUSTING!

We get it. We understand what you're going through. We see it in your faces. We hear it in your voices. We read it in your tweets. But we also see that the biggest difference between your pain and ours is that whiteness is not resilient. You are stuck in your loops of disbelief or anger and that's all you talk about. You go on and on about how shitty things are. How sorry you are for the behavior of other white people. You moan, you whine, and of course you cry...there are a lot of tears.

**BUT THAT IS ALL.**
**YOU DO NOT TAKE MEANINGFUL ACTION.**

So on this day. A day that so many, *on both sides*, are hoping will be the defining moment regarding the essential nature and character of the United States, I thought it would be the perfect time to help anti-racist white people process and get out of their feelings and join the rest of us in creating an identity for the United States that it was not designed to have.

## 1. Denial

Denial, let's be honest, is where most white people, in the United States, fall. They continue to sit in disbelief at the telling of our stories. These are the individuals who know something is different but are not yet ready to accept that their privilege, if they will even admit to having any, was gained as a result of oppressing and annihilating others. They are working hard to reconcile what they hear and see in the media or real life with the intentional lack of historical knowledge they need to make any sense of this new understanding. These are the individuals who pepper us with requests for data, they #notallwhitepeople and #alllivesmatter us because any other responses would mean acknowledging their own ignorance and role, intentional or otherwise, in maintaining the house of white supremacy.

285

## 2. Anger

Anger is one of the two stages where white people get stuck and boy do you get angry. Every other word out of your mouths is "fight this" and "fight that". It makes sense to want to fight but what many of you are unaware of is that your calls to fight seldom will make you the victim. What usually happens is that your anger triggers the anger of other white people and they in turn focus their anger onto the very communities of marginalized individuals you are angrily working to protect. We've increasingly seen this play out in examples such as "Black man beaten in Charlottesville found not guilty of assaulting white supremacist"[1]; "'whites don't shoot whites,' suspected gunman told man after killing 2 black customers at Kentucky Kroger"[2]; "U.S. militia groups head to border, stirred by Trump's call to arms"[3]; and "when the dreaded 'other' is an angry white man"[4] to name a few. White people must understand that although anger is a normal stage in the grieving process, your anger does not put you in danger but threatens the lives and well-being of the most vulnerable members of our society.

---

1  https://www.washingtonpost.com/local/black-man-beaten-in-charlottesville-found-not-guilty-of-assaulting-white-supremacist/2018/03/16/92160a88-288f-11e8-b79d-f3d931db7f68_story.html

2  https://www.washingtonpost.com/local/black-man-beaten-in-charlottesville-found-not-guilty-of-assaulting-white-supremacist/2018/03/16/92160a88-288f-11e8-b79d-f3d931db7f68_story.html

3  https://www.washingtonpost.com/world/national-security/us-militia-groups-head-to-border-stirred-by-trumps-call-to-arms/2018/11/03/ff96826c-decf-11e8-b3f0-62607289efee_story.html

4  https://www.cnn.com/2018/11/05/us/angry-white-man-john-blake/index.html

## 3. Bargaining

Let me be honest, although I am very aware of the stages and the need for individuals to move through them at their own pace, bargaining is the stage where I lose my patience with white people. This is the stage where you really work my nerves because this is where you center yourself, often to the detriment of those communities who are actually in harms way. You are so into your guilt for "not knowing" that instead of channeling your newfound understanding into learning and taking action, you position yourself as a martyr or, god forbid, an ally, and every conversation is about you, how badly you feel for not being aware of white supremacy or even the level of your own privilege. THIS IS NOT ABOUT YOU! I get it. You're upset. But please stop making your shit to unpack and deal with, the emotional labor of others, particularly individuals whose lived experiences are steeped in the oppression of white supremacy.

## 4. Depression

Depression. Now this is a big one because this is the other stage that white people get stuck in because working to dismantle a system of white supremacy seems like an impossible and overwhelming effort. How does one even start to work on attacking this goal? So many of us are used to instant gratification of getting to the "win" that for many, not seeing a way to an easy "win" sends you into a place of "why bother". Why bother? Because our lives depend on you. We need your effort, your energy, your ideas, and your resources to make meaningful, long-lasting change and we need it like yesterday. Yes, this is a daunting undertaking but really think about the alternative.

Although you may only be a witness to the atrocities that white supremacy historically and continues to inflict on marginalized communities, what you are also beginning to notice is that you, as a white person, are increasingly being impacted by its negative outcomes. This is because white supremacy is a parasite that has now started to eat its host...WHITENESS.

## 5. Acceptance

Acceptance! Finally! It is only when you are able to accept that as a white person, you have unfairly benefitted from the unearned privileges stolen from others, that you are of any help to those already on the ground, working to dismantle white supremacy. Your effort is an important component of this work and we need you to do your part. We need you to not wait around looking for orders but to actively engage by asking "how can I help?", "where do you need me?", "who can I connect you to?", and "how can I fund this?" to name a few. It is important for you to also check your privilege to ensure that you are not stepping into roles where you are not qualified or that are occupied by others. You should be doing everything you can to amplify and lift the people, voices, and initiatives of those with limited or no privilege, while remaining in the background.

Also, if you're serious about dismantling white supremacy, check out the Being Antiracist events. Take this opportunity to learn the basics of being Antiracist, while minimizing the potential for harm your whiteness has on others, as you learn. **Again, let me state, that this is not about you because the work we are doing, when giving the support we need, benefits us all.**

# The Profit Without Oppression Glossary

*"Knowledge is power and ignorance is no longer an excuse for causing harm."*

*- Kim Crayton -*

## Anti-Blackness
Anti-Blackness is the term used to describe a specific prejudice toward Black folx.

## Antiracism
Antiracism is the action of actively recognizing and countering racist systems, racial prejudice, and racial oppression.

## Apolitical
Not being involved in politics or having interest in it.

## Business

A product or service is not a business; it's just a product or service. You're building a business once you move beyond the minutia of developing a functioning product or service to operationalizing your core values into policies, procedures, and processes, and enlisting the support of stakeholders.

## Capitalism

An economic and political system in which a country's trade and industry are controlled by private owners for profit rather than by the state.

## CEO vs. COO

A CEO is at the top of company management and oversees long-term operations and strategy for the business. A COO is second in command and focuses on day-to-day operations and current company functions.

## Compromise vs. Collaborate

When two parties meet at a compromise, both parties give up something in exchange, leaving neither party fully satisfied. When the two parties collaborate, they work together to ensure both parties' needs are met. They end up creating something together that they never could alone.

## Convenience vs. Conscience

All too often, folx find themselves when engaging with systems, institutions, and policies designed to privilege the few at the expense of the many having to make "ethical/moral" decisions on whether to participate and if so, how. We run elaborate mental calculations to help us live with a multitude of decisions related to the convenience of using a product or service versus a laundry list of factors on how doing so impacts our internal compasses and engaging in an ever-increasingly connected world only exacerbates our decision making processes.

For example, when deciding whether to use a new product or service, many people find themselves in situations where they are attempting to determine how much "harm" they are willing to tolerate or be complicit in order to meet their needs.

# DEI

DEI stands for Diversity, Equity, and Inclusion. DEI is a practice that is used within certain businesses, companies, and institutions to increase diversity, commit to practices that ensure equity, and create inclusive spaces.

## Diversity

Diversity refers to an environment that is occupied with folx of different social, ethnic, gender, and other backgrounds.

## Explicit vs. Tacit

When something is explicit, it is said or written clearly where there is no room for doubt as to its meaning. When something is tacit, it means that it is knowledge that is implied or expected to be understood without stating it.

## Gender Nonconforming

(also called GNC, or gender atypical) Involves not conforming to a given culture's gender norm expectations. Gender nonconforming is a phrase for someone whose gender expression doesn't match their society's prescribed gender roles or gender norms for their gender identity. Gender nonconformity transgresses societal or psychological expectations for perceived gender assignment through presentation, behavior, identity, or other means. A person who is gender nonconforming may or may not consider themselves transgender or even LGBT at all.

Gender nonconformity is a broad term that can include transgender as well as cisgender people.

## Inclusion

Inclusion in business is the practice or policy of including folx who have historically not been included by providing opportunities, resources, and environments that actively work to incorporate them and make them feel safe.

## Information vs. Knowledge vs. Wisdom

Information is accessible to anyone, knowledge is internalizing that information, and wisdom is leveraging knowledge, along with lived experience, in an effective way.

## Learning Organization

"An organization where people continually expand their capacity to create the results they truly desire, where new and expansive patterns of thinking are nurtured, where collective aspiration is set free, and where people are continually learning how to learn together." The Fifth Discipline: The Art & Practice of The Learning Organization, Peter Senge

## Lived Experience

Knowledge gained through personal experiences and choices. This knowledge may be unique to a person or present within a particular group of people.

## Marginalized

To relegate to an unimportant or powerless position within a society or group. This is about how folx are treated within systems, institutions, and policies designed to exclude them.

## Micro-aggression vs. Professional Violence

A micro-aggression is "a comment or action that subtly and often unconsciously or unintentionally expresses a prejudiced attitude toward a member of a marginalized group (such as a racial minority)."

Professional violence is any "intense, turbulent, or furious and often destructive action or force" in a professional situation that leverages the systems, institutions, and policies of white supremacy against a member of a marginalized group.

## Mission-Driven vs. Profit-Driven

Mission-driven businesses focus on a particular purpose that they stand for. Mission-driven is historically associated with nonprofits but may also include for-profit businesses. A profit-driven business is one that focuses on extracting as much profit as it can.

## Multipotentialite

A multipotentialite is a person who has many interdisciplinary interests. They have several and very diverse aptitudes.

## Non-Binary

Relating to or being a person who identifies with or expresses a gender identity that is neither entirely male nor entirely female.

## Offboarding

Offboarding is the separation of an employee from a company. It is the reverse of onboarding and is a process that is used to ease the transition for both former employee and employer.

## Oppression

The exercise of power or authority used to unjustly and/or cruelly control or treat someone or a group of people.

## Organizational Learning

A process used by a business or institution to improve itself over time through creating, recording, and transferring knowledge throughout the organization. This is different from a Learning Organization.

## Policy vs. Process vs. Procedure

Policy refers to the rules or guidelines an organization has in place to determine its course of action and maintain efficiency. Processes are the activities used to produce a product, service or experience. While processes are broad overviews, a procedure is a specific set of instructions to accomplish a part of the production of a product or service.

## Powell Memo

A confidential memorandum written by Lewis F. Powell in 1971 to Eugene B. Sydnor, Jr., chair of the Education Committee of the U.S. Chamber of Commerce. The memo, titled "Attack on American Free Enterprise System," described a system through which businesses should counter what he called "a broad attack" (See Appendix 1). This counterattack would be executed through corporate domination of Americans' views of business, politics, and law. Powell advocated for surveillance of textbooks, television programs, and other content to "purge" left-wing ideology as well as the funding of a "media outreach program" to counter it. The memo was leaked a year later and is credited with shaping aspects of U.S Capitalism.

## Privilege

A benefit, advantage, or right that is only accessible or available to a specific person or group of people.

## Profit

A financial gain or benefit after an investment or expenses.

## Psychological Safety

"It is a shared belief held by members of a team that the team is safe for interpersonal risk-taking. It describes a team climate characterized by interpersonal trust and mutual respect in which people are comfortable being themselves." – Amy Edmondson, 1999

## Racism

Discrimination or prejudice toward a person or group based on their race or ethnic group, as well as a belief that people of different racial groups have different characteristics or qualities that are then used to distinguish the racial group as inferior to the other.

## Retention

Retention is the continued keeping or possession of something. Retention in the job space is holding onto employees, suppliers, and other stakeholders.

## Risk Management/Crisis Management

Preparing policies and procedures that can be utilized to prevent problems and in case of an issue or emergency. This includes policies that record, review, and check records and data to prevent errors and issues, as well as policies to handle issues if they do occur.

## Soft Skills

Skills that are applicable to all professional settings. They are core skills that can include problem-solving, teamwork, work ethic, leadership, communication, and more. Referring to these vital skills as "soft" often leads to problematic outcomes, the same with "non-technical" because they aren't valued as "must-haves." In a knowledge economy, any leaders making this error are creating barriers to their ability to leverage organizational knowledge for innovation, differentiation, and competitive advantage.

## Stakeholder vs. Shareholders

A shareholder is a person who owns shares of stock in a company and, therefore, holds ownership in part of a public company. A stakeholder is someone who has an interest in the business and may be affected by the company's choices, policies, and activities. EX: employees, suppliers, etc.

## Technical vs. Technology

We have a tendency to mistakenly use these words interchangeably as synonyms. Technical is related to a particular subject, art, craft, or its techniques, while technology is related to the application of scientific knowledge for practical purposes, especially industry. Technical is simply specialized knowledge, which many folx within an organization possess within their specific domains, i.e., HR, marketing, customer support, etc., while technology is a function of applying that knowledge. What we create by labeling some folx within an organization as "technical" while labeling others as "non-technical" communicates value, which then gets played out at various touchpoints and circumstances in designing organizational policies, procedures, and processes via pay, retention/promotion, shifting economic factors, etc.

## Transgender

Of, relating to, or being a person whose gender identity differs from the sex the person had or was identified as having at birth.

## Underrepresented

A group is underrepresented if they are present within a space at disproportionately low numbers.

## Welcoming

Hospitable, accessible, and cordial

## White Supremacy

The belief that white people are superior to other races, especially the Black race, and that they should be centered and dominating within society while excluding other racial groups.

# Index

## I: KNOW THYSELF

- A blueprint for a house has the floor, walls, and a roof in common; it's the foundation. But the design and materials of those things can be as unique as the needs of those who live there.
- An exercise is self-awareness: White dudes review your resume/CV. How many roles have you gained access to WITHOUT meeting all the qualifications?
- Antiracist economist
- Audience: nonprofit and for-profit
- Being "antiracist" is a verb, a practice.
- Black women are the moral compass. Find the darkest women in any community for practical solutions to many of our problems.
- Briefly share the #causeascene story for context.
- Challenging the status quo of assigning credit or blame
- Creating a common language
- Ensuring welcoming and psychological safety from the invitation to salutation
- Everyone has their own internalized white supremacy and anti-Blackness to address because we've ALL been indoctrinated in the same S/I/P.
- Ex. Part 1: Leading for Inclusion [PP]
- Folx have to be willing to engage in hard, uncomfortable conversations.

- Format: Stop that, this is why, and this is what we're going to do instead
- Guided principles
- How to apologize and make amends
- Ideology/belief
- Intention without strategy is chaos.
- I want to address and challenge white supremacy & anti-Blackness without ever mentioning it.
- Knowledge is power, and ignorance is no longer an excuse for causing harm.
- Lack of inclusion is a risk/crisis-management issue.
- Letters to the Antiracist Entrepreneur
- Lived experience
- Mediocre and unremarkable whiteness
- "Mission-Driven" vs. "Profit-Driven" vs. "Hybrid": All need to operationalize policies, procedures, and policies.
- No more new wine into old wineskins.

## Part 1: "Know Thy Self" — Being an Antiracist Entrepreneur

- Part 1: Know Thy Self [floor], Part 2: Know Thy Organization [walls], Part 3: Know Thy Community [roof]
- Part 1: Managing Tech content flow Part 2: 6-Step Strategy Part 3: Organizational Hospitality
- Prioritize the most vulnerable
- Profit Without Oppression now asks the question: "Is it possible to advance; improve without oppressing the world around us?"
- Questioning humanity/ right to exist

- Replace Employer or Become an Employer, both require the operationalization of policies, procedures, and policies.
- Rules of engagement
- Supremacy-FREE, Coercion-FREE, Discrimination-FREE, xploitation-FREE
- Tech is not neutral, nor is it apolitical.
- The Future Is FREE.
- The master's tools will never dismantle the master's house.
- The Pandemic Exposed systems, institutions, and policies of harm.
- The Powell Memo
- The racial reckoning
- The secret to change is to focus all your energy, not on fighting the old but on building the new.
- This book is designed to provide a strategy for developing a consistent, demonstrated, antiracist practice.
- This book is for folx who'd like to stop being complicit in the harming of others.
- This work isn't about who's racist [over the years, I've made that clear]. It's about developing a consistent, demonstrated antiracist practice.
- We will make mistakes because we're trying to create an experience that was never meant to exist.
- We're trying to create a world that was never supposed to exist.


## II: KNOW THY ORGANIZATION

- 6-Step business development strategy
- A product/service is not a business...It's a product/service.

- Building Commonalities: Floor [Define CV] Walls [Operationalize CV] Roof [Measure CV]
- Building shared vision
- Ex. Part 2. Business Development Lab
- Learning organization
- Mental models
- One of the appeals of owning a franchise is the established policies, procedures, and processes.
- Our organizational Stakeholders are [listed in order of priority]: 1. Those who work for you 2. Those who partner with you 3. Those who buy from you 4. Those who are impacted by you  5. Those who invest in you
- Personal mastery
- Prioritizes Stakeholder Value, Community, minimizing harm & the most vulnerable
- Shareholder value vs. Stakeholder value
- Systems thinking
- Team learning
- These commonalities are not new. The difference is developing a CV from supremacy-, coercion-, discrimination-, and exploitation-free framework.
- You can't manage what you can't measure.

## III:  KNOW THY COMMUNITY

- Applicant selection
- Application design
- CEO=COO
- Compensation Structure Baseline + # of Roles and Responsibilities
- DEI Removed from HR; DEI = HR
- Evaluation

- Exiting HR/Legal, i.e., NDAs
- Exit interview
- Feedback on the onboarding processes
- Giving and receiving feedback
- Interview process
- Job announcement
- Job description
- Joining HR/Legal
- Knowledge Organizational Sharing [Explicit/Tacit]
- Knowledge Transfer [Capture Tacit before it walks out the door]
- Leadership & Management
- Make sure that communities within communities are not pitted against each other for attention and/or resources.
- Making an offer
- Managing your feelings
- Mentoring
- My issues with "Move fast and break things."
- Offboarding
- Offer negotiation
- Onboarding
- Organization learning
- Organizations are NOT families...this is manipulative.
- Orientation
- Peer guide
- Probation
- Promotion
- Recruiting
- References
- Resignation
- Retaining
- Shareholder vs. stakeholders
- Termination
- The Great Resignation

- Training and development
- White women are not diversity

## Whiteness in Marginalized Spaces

- All speech/opinions/perspectives are not equal.
- Building a team with the "right" people is one thing. Getting those individuals to work together in ways that are strategic, innovative, competitive, and profitable is quite another. Getting your team to value collaboration and to share what they know/learn with others ensures that organizational leaders are able to leverage the knowledge and skills they need to make decisions that matter.
- Collaboration cannot be forced; it must be encouraged by removing barriers and building trust.
- Ex. Part 3: Organizational Hospitality Check
- From domain expert to managing the roles and responsibilities of others
- In office vs. remote
- Instant gratification vs. long-term strategy
- It's not a pipeline issue.
- My issue with "move fast and break things" is that rarely does leadership stop to ask: What did we break, how did we break it, who did we harm, and how do we make amends?
- Organizational development that's rooted in prioritizing minimizing harm & the most vulnerable should be approached as community development.
- Organizational Hospitality & the 5 Stakeholders
- Profit Without Oppression prioritizes * IMPACT over INTENTION * Welcoming and psychological safety * Lived experience over theory * Authentic conversations

    * Hopefulness * Strategic action * "Kind" over "nice" *
    Community over individualism * Equity over equality.

- Public, private, nonprofit, for-profit, and governmental
- PWO is the lens through which you view the business landscape...every resource, relationship, and responsibility.
- Stop looking for simple solutions to complex problems.
- The "soft skills" myth
- The myth of "the culture wars"
- This is not a magic bullet, and it's hard work.
- This is not a one-size-fits-all solution; it is an organizational orientation.
- This is NOT a system to be implemented. It's a lens through which one makes decisions and guides behavior.

# About the Author

As the Antiracist Economist, Kim Crayton is dedicated to building a future that Is Supremacy-, Coercion-, Discrimination-, and Exploitation-FREE. Formerly known for #causeascene, she used her platform to call out harm and the facade of inclusion, often consulting with tech companies that were experiencing "challenges" when it came  to ensuring the welcoming and psychological safety of their work environment.

After years of the status quo, Kim has shifted. She is no longer putting out fires and is ready to focus her time and efforts on moving forward. Having worked many years as an educator, she decided to become the mentor she wished she'd had. Using her own lived experience to guide her, Kim has been actively working to build businesses that model Profit Without Oppression by sharing knowledge and helping others develop skills in ways that accommodate the masses. In doing so, Kim is laying the foundation for a Future that is Hopeful, Authentic, and Strategic in Action...Are you in?

## Connect with Kim Crayton

Instagram: https://www.instagram.com/kimcrayton1/

Facebook: https://www.facebook.com/KimCraytonLLC

LinkedIn: https://www.linkedin.com/in/kimcrayton/

Twitter: https://twitter.com/KimCrayton1

Mastodon: https://dair-community.social/@KimCrayton1

Website: kimcrayton.com

Email: info@profitwithoutoppression.com

CPSIA information can be obtained
at www.ICGtesting.com
Printed in the USA
BVHW051835090123
655919BV00008B/43